Writing a Successful College Application Essay

Fourth Edition • George Ehrenhaft

BARRON'S

For Dave, Ellie, and Sylvia

About the Author

George Ehrenhaft, a graduate of Columbia College and Ohio State University, has helped students write successful college application essays for over three decades. He is the former head of the English Department at Mamaroneck High School (NY) and resides in Moraga, California.

© Copyright 2008 by Barron's Educational Series, Inc.
Prior editions © Copyright 2000, 1993, 1987 by Barron's Educational Series, Inc.

All inquiries should be addressed to:

Barron's Educational Series, Inc.
250 Wireless Boulevard
Hauppauge, New York 11788
www.barronseduc.com

Library of Congress Catalog Card No. 2007043441

ISBN-13: 978-0-7641-3637-5
ISBN-10: 0-7641-3637-2

Library of Congress Cataloging-in-Publication Data

Ehrenhaft, George.
    Writing a successful college application essay : the key to college admission / George Ehrenhaft.—4th ed.
        p. cm.
    Includes index.
    ISBN-13: 978-0-7641-3637-5 (alk. paper)
    ISBN-10: 0-7641-3637-2 (alk. paper)
    1. College applications. 2. Exposition (Rhetoric) 3. Universities and colleges—Admission. 4. Academic writing. I. Title.

    LB2351.5.E37 2008
    378.1'662—dc22

                                                                    2007043441

PRINTED IN THE UNITED STATES OF AMERICA
9 8 7 6

Table of Contents

ACKNOWLEDGMENTS

Scores of people have contributed to this book. Many are the high school students who populated my English classes for over three decades. They taught *me* far more than I could ever have taught them about the craft of writing. From their stumbling but sincere writing efforts, I learned what it takes to make words clear, interesting, and correct. The lessons they taught me echo throughout these pages.

A college application essay offers a writing teacher the ultimate high. Perhaps for the first time, students write something that counts for more than just a grade in school. They see that skill in writing can make a difference in their lives, that words empower them to disturb the universe. For showing me the way, I'm indebted to Rose Scotch, Michael DiGennaro, and the late Susan Freeman. I also wish to thank Ileen Gottesfeld, Paul Martin, and Ettore Piraino for contributing their students' essays to the book.

I'm especially grateful to the dozens of students who consented to have their college essays reproduced—in whole or in part—throughout this volume. Most of the essays were written in Mamaroneck (NY) High School, but they also come from students attending Mahopac High School, Scarsdale High School, White Plains High School, John Jay High School in Cross River, NY, Horace Greeley High School in Chappaqua, NY, and the Berkshire School in Sheffield, Massachusetts.

The gracious volunteers in Mamaroneck's College Information Center gave expert help and provided a site for fruitful discussions with college admissions representatives from across the nation. A heartfelt thanks, too, to the dozens of deans and directors of admission who described how essays are used in making admissions decisions. I also appreciate the help of Bob O'Sullivan at Barron's.

I save my biggest hug for Al Greenberg, formerly at the American School in Milan, Italy. As Al talked to me about writing application essays, I realized that he probably should have written this book. In a sense, I became another of the countless students who have benefited from his insights and experience as a counselor.

Finally, to my wife Susan: Your support has been incalculable.

G.E.

Every college and university should ask
prospective students to submit an essay as
part of their application for admission, not only
to underline the importance of writing, but also as a
means of learning more about the needs as well as
the strengths of students.

—A recommendation from
*College: The Undergraduate
Experience in America,* a study of
education by the Carnegie Foundation for
the Advancement of Teaching

1 ADMIT? DEFER? REJECT?

Put on a pair of virtual reality goggles for a moment and place yourself behind the desk of a college admissions officer, reviewing applications for next year's freshman class. You've read about 45 applications today, and you are down to your last three. Your colleagues have gone home. It's dark outside, and you are tired and hungry. The stack of rejected applications on your desk reaches almost to the level of your aching eyes. The "maybe" pile is half as tall. A wire basket marked "yes!" holds another stack barely three inches high.

At eight o'clock tomorrow the admissions committee will need your decisions. You carry an awesome burden on your shoulders—the destiny of real, live people. Each person comes from a good high school. Teachers and counselors have sent warm endorsements. None of the three has alumni connections—they'll sink or swim on their own. It's in your hands. What will you recommend? Admit? Wait-list? Reject?

Jeff G's papers show you that he has taken tough courses in high school and that he will graduate in the top ten percent of his class. You also note an SAT score near 2100 and participation in school life as a yearbook staffer, cross-country runner, and co-captain of the debate team.

> As an admissions officer, you carry an awesome burden on your shoulders—the destiny of real, live people.

Then you come to the essay question, which asks applicants to describe an important personal experience and explain its significance. Jeff's response is rather uninspired. It makes the point that involvement in various high school activities has taught him to be a serious-minded, hard-working, and responsible person. In college he expects to study hard and earn good grades.

Kathy E's application boasts several achievements in foreign languages. You observe that Kathy has won school certificates in Spanish and French and that she has also studied Chinese. She plans to major in languages and hopes someday to work for the U.S. Department of State. Her overall average is 90 and her SAT score is 1950. In school she joined the language clubs and helped to publish a foreign language newspaper.

Kathy's essay contains a list of European countries she visited during the last two summers and makes the point that, although travel is broadening and fun, there's no place like home.

Pat McM's application shows that he earned an 86 average in a generally rigorous academic program, including an AP history course. His ACT score is not distinguished, but still within the range for your college. Pat acted in high school drama productions, played the saxophone in the jazz band, and in 11th grade devoted considerable time to Students for a Clean Environment.

To answer the essay question, Pat wrote an imaginary conversation with God after the ozone layer had been completely destroyed and only a few human beings were left on the planet.

Three good students, three qualified candidates for admission to your college. A high average and varied activities strengthen Jeff's application. Kathy's special interest in language commends her strongly. Pat's commitment to outside activities compensates for his marginal numbers.

How Colleges Decide

After checking your grades and courses, each college will take a slightly different path. Some turn to your recommendations from counselors and teachers, others to test results. Although nearly all colleges tell you to take the SAT or ACT, they don't all give the scores equal weight.

> You won't spring to life for the admissions committee without a thoughtful, well-written essay.

How you spent time outside of class is crucial, too, because colleges seek people who have charged full speed ahead into life. They want students who will participate, who will help shape the life on campus or in the community. They judge you according to the depth of your involvement, not by the number of activities you've joined.

The reputation of your secondary school also counts. Colleges know which schools habitually send out high-achieving, energetic learners. In addition, colleges like a geographic blend, often favoring candidates from distant regions of the country.

An alumni connection often helps, and a cordial interview also adds strength to your record, especially when you travel to the campus to meet the dean of admissions.

> Typically, an effective essay can go a long way to offset a mediocre SAT score.

Each section of a college application adds another dimension to your portrait, but you won't spring to life for the admissions committee without a thoughtful, well-written essay. The essay serves a window into your mind and personality: Unlike an A– in chemistry or an 80 in English, it reveals your uniqueness—what you think about, what drives you, and to what you aspire. Of course, it demonstrates your writing ability, too. The gift of saying what you want to say the way you want to say it can compensate for a weakness in almost any other part of the application. Typically, an effective essay can go a long way to offset a mediocre SAT score. In fact, if most applicants poured as much sweat into their essays as they do into college test preparation, admissions officials would be inundated with volumes of first-rate reading.

What would you tell Jeff, Kathy, and Pat? Admit? Defer? Reject? The majority of colleges in the United States would probably admit all three without hesitation, glad to have attracted applicants of such high caliber. But more selective schools would screen them with agonizing care before deciding. An admissions committee may assign numerical ratings to each candidate's academic and personal qualities. Two committee members might read each folder and make a recommendation. Difficult folders are often passed around the committee for a group decision. At the University of Chicago, up to seven people have been known to read a single application.

Perhaps only 300 of nearly 2,000 four-year colleges in the United States choose their students with such agonizing care. In recent years, the process has become increasingly complex. In fact, America's most competitive colleges and universities are turning away more applicants now than at any time in their history. Why? Because they are receiving more applications than ever before. First, there are more high school seniors applying to college— about two million a year. Also, the average number of applications per student has doubled in the last decade. In 1999, four to six

Only 300 of nearly 2,000 colleges in the U.S. receive four or more applications for each place in the freshman class.

applications was the standard. Now, it's not unusual for high school seniors to apply to a dozen or more colleges.

Between 2000 and 2007, for example, applications to Middlebury College jumped from 4,400 to nearly 7,200. Kenyon College received 2,000 applications in 2001 and 4,600 in 2007. During those seven years, the number of students applying to the University of Vermont surged from 7,400 to 19,000. More than 50,000 students applied for admission to the class of 2011 at UCLA, almost twice the number who applied for the class of 2007.

As a consequence of this application explosion, admission rates at selective colleges have tumbled. In the 1990s, for example, Pomona College in California accepted nearly half its applicants. In the spring of 2007, it took only 15 percent. During the same period, Lehigh's rate of acceptance fell from 60 to 31 percent, and Bowdoin's from 40 to 18.5 percent. In 2007, Columbia became one of the most selective colleges in the country. Of 18,081 applicants, only 1,618 were accepted, an acceptance rate of 8.9 percent.

Regardless of the numbers, however, the screening of applicants is never done haphazardly. Colleges immediately eliminate anyone who clearly can't do the work. "In general," says Muhlenberg's dean of admissions, Christopher Hooker-Haring, "students do a pretty good job of matching themselves up with colleges." As a result, 85 to 90 percent are academically qualified and survive the first cut, although admissions officials often turn down overqualified candidates because colleges prefer not to pursue candidates who are almost certain to decline their invitations to attend. Next, a college may pick out a small group of superstars, from presidential scholars to world-class swimmers. The balance of candidates are left in what Harry Bauld, a former admissions representative at Brown and Columbia, has termed "the gray area." These applicants, Bauld says, are "in the ball park" but still far from being accepted. Faced with large numbers of good scholastic records—like those submitted by Jeff, Kathy, and Pat—admissions officials make decisions using what Karl M. Furstenberg, dean of admissions at Dartmouth calls "the intangibles," qualities that don't show up on a transcript and can't be listed in a résumé. "This makes our job harder," claims Furstenberg. "It forces us to look at critical thinking." And nowhere is an applicant's level of thinking more evident than in the application essay.

The Application Essay

"The essay can make the difference between a *wait-list* and an *admit* or a *wait-list* and a *deny*," says Jennifer Stein, who reads candidates' essays in the Connecticut College admissions office. "It can tip the balance, giving students an extra edge, or it can work against them." Jonathan Reider, Senior Associate Director of Admissions at Stanford, concurs. The essay can play "a crucial role in deciding who among well-qualified applicants are the most compelling candidates for admission."

> "The essay can tip the balance," says Connecticut College.

Around the conference table in admissions offices, the essay often serves as the wild card, the piece of an application that may give an edge to a student like Pat McM. Writing a conversation with God shows that Pat has the courage to take intellectual and creative risks. Pat's approach is unique, and it confirms his interest in environmental issues. That he wrote a dialogue may suggest that his drama experience has left an enduring mark on the way he thinks. In short, he put himself into his writing.

On the other hand, Jeff G and Kathy E didn't. Both wrote proper, but boring, essays, which couldn't be distinguished from hundreds of others. Jeff's "what-I-did-in-high-school-and-what-I-learned-from-it" approach is common and uninspired. So is Kathy's conclusion. Kathy roamed Europe, but brought back a cliché. By submitting dull essays, both Jeff and Kathy have tarnished otherwise sterling records and have jeopardized their chances of getting into a selective college.

Why Colleges Ask for an Essay

If you're wondering why colleges require an essay, welcome to the club. Countless students just like you have asked the same question. After all, you've already written an essay for the SAT or the ACT Writing Test. Furthermore, colleges have a fairly accurate sense of your essay-writing ability from your grades in English and other courses that require essay writing.

Yet, you've been handed still another essay assignment. By asking for an essay or two, colleges are telling you that writing well is important in college—and in life. But more to the point, they're giving you an opportunity to show them who you really are. Virtually every admissions official in the country will tell you that the course grades, teacher recommendations, and test scores all count heavily, but an essay projects a clearer sense of what makes you tick, what turns you on and off, and what you stand for. In other words, it's the only place on the application where you have the freedom to put your personal qualities front and center. As Dean Hooker-Haring of Muhlenberg College puts it, the essay enables you to "reach out and grab an admissions officer by the lapels, and say, 'Here I am! This is why I belong at your college!'"

In fact, most colleges tell you on the application: "We want to get to know you as well as we can." They ask you to present yourself honestly and encourage you to write an essay in which you avoid trying to appear to be someone you think they would want as a student in their campus. The truth is, they want you to show yourself as the person you really are.

To help you bring out your uniqueness, many colleges ask a variety of questions—some creative, some off-the-wall, some inspiring, some provocative, but all of them dead serious about finding out what you have inside your head and heart. Prospective members of American University's class of 2012 were asked to imagine themselves as editors of a major news magazine and to write the cover story for the issue dated January 1, 2025. Applicants to Bennington are invited to invent and write a mission statement for an organization formed to solve a political, social, or global problem. Those with a more mechanical bent are asked to explain the forces exerted on a broom leaning against a wall. Admissions officials at the University of Pennsylvania realized that by asking the same old questions, they got the same old answers. Therefore, they replaced a conventional "definition of success" question with a more engaging one: "You've just written a 300-page autobiography; please submit page 217 with this application."

Most colleges, however, ask more traditional questions. Typical among them is this one from Columbia:

> Write an essay which conveys to the reader a sense of who you are. Possible topics may include, but are not limited to, experiences which have shaped your life, the circumstances of your upbringing, your most meaningful intellectual achievement, the way you see the world—the people in it, events great and small, everyday life—or any personal theme which appeals to your imagination.

At any college that requires an application essay (the vast majority don't), officials read them attentively because they're on the lookout for the best, most promising, and most vibrant students they can find. At some colleges the essay is passed along to academic advisors, who use it to help students plan their freshman programs. In addition, a college can often tell from an essay whether the applicant is eligible for a restricted scholarship or some other type of special aid. Eventually, essays may end up in the files available to teachers, administrators, and counselors.

Write Your Way into College

Demands for writing essays vary from college to college. Hundreds of colleges—among them Boston University, Northwestern, Princeton, Colorado College, and the University of the Pacific—require one essay, although many ask you to write additional paragraphs in response to specific questions on topics such as your interests, goals, and achievements. The Common Application, used by several hundred colleges, calls for only one essay, but scores of those colleges—such as Amherst, Rice, and the University of San Francisco—ask for a second or even third essay to be written in response to questions on their own supplemental applications. Rensselaer requires two essays, but the topic for one of them varies according to the applicant's anticipated major. Future dentists write on different subjects than future architects. Some colleges, such as Mt. Holyoke, Sarah Lawrence, and Hampshire, ask applicants to submit not only an essay but an analytical paper written for a high school class, complete with teachers' comments and a grade.

In the admissions process, a perfect essay—even if such a thing existed—doesn't make up for less-than-brilliant grades or a transcript full of easy high school courses. A study by the National Association of College Admissions Counselors found that most of America's selective colleges choose students by their grades in college prep courses, recommendations, and their *ability to write the application essay*. In fact, over half of the colleges give the essay "considerable" to "moderate" weight in admission decisions. Jennifer Blair, an associate director of admissions at Marlboro College, ranks the essay as the second most important criterion after the applicant's academic record. That is, after

> By giving the essay all you've got, you could actually write your way into college.

grades and difficulty of course load. At Bennington, Bryn Mawr, and Smith, where the essay carries as much weight as any other part of the application, committees discuss applicants' writing at length. When admissions people convene for all-day sessions at Wesleyan, they guard against carelessness by taking frequent breaks. An application that surfaces late in the afternoon is read as respectfully as one at nine o'clock in the morning.

Although finding your way into the right college may seem like traversing a labyrinth, over a million students make the trip every year. At times the admissions system may appear fickle and unpredictable, almost beyond understanding. Yet, it works. As a college-bound student, you took your first steps toward your destination years ago when you learned to read and write and to compute numbers. You've studied, worked, and contributed in some way to your school and community. You've taken the SAT or ACT and established your school record. You narrowed your college preferences, and perhaps had an interview or two.

In your essay, prove to the admissions staff that you're too good to turn down.

By the time you fill in your name on your first application, the facts about you—for better or worse—are in. You can't change them. However, the opportunities in your essay are wide open. In your answers to the essay questions you have the chance to shine brighter than your competition, to prove that you deserve a place in next year's freshman class. Let the essay work for you. The remainder of this book will show you how.

2 AN ESSAY THAT WORKS

In a survey about "life's ten most anxious moments," a majority of high school seniors agreed that getting up to talk in front of a group provoked the most anxiety. Second was applying to college, especially writing the essay.

It's easy to see why. The two tasks—addressing a group and composing an essay for a college application—have a lot in common. In both cases success depends on how well you present yourself, what you have to say, and how effectively you convey your message. Few people don't feel at least a little stage fright before facing an audience, and it's equally natural to feel edgy about filling up an empty sheet of paper with an essay that could clear or block your entry to your college of choice.

But, if you can be objective about it, you don't need to get into a sweat over your essay. Once you have a handle on what colleges expect, once you know the pitfalls to avoid and are psyched to do a good job, the application essay won't be all that intimidating. Yes, it will take time and energy—but with any luck, the payoff will be well worth it.

Essay Tips

As you go about preparing, writing, and editing your essay, keep in mind the following basic tips. Although some of them are pretty obvious, they have helped countless college applicants conquer their essay-writing anxiety.

- **Start early**. The summer between junior and senior year is perfect. Free from the pressures of school and other obligations, use your days in the sun to think about a topic. Test out your essay ideas informally with chat groups and other people whose judgment you trust. Use the time to read books like this one and to study successful sample essays found in print or online. (*Turn to pages 39–89 for more on what to write about.*)
- **Cast aside preconceptions of what a college wants**. Don't assume that admissions officials want anything but an honest piece of writing that gives them an accurate glimpse of who you are. (*See page 11 for more on the perils of trying too hard to please the college.*)

- **Answer the question**. You'd be surprised at how many applicants miss the point of the question and dash off marginally-related essays.

- **Avoid clichés**. That is, don't write the same essay that other applicants are likely to write. Rather, devise something new and fresh and engaging, something that will help you stand out in a crowd of hundreds, or even thousands, of other applicants. (*See page 15 for tips on writing a unique essay.*)

- **Choose an appropriate tone**. Don't pretend to be someone you are not. Avoid boasting, whining, groveling, self-pity, and making excuses. You are a high school senior on the verge of adulthood. Act and sound like one. (*See page 19 for tips on the boasting problem.*)

- **Write a well-organized, detailed essay that focuses on a single main idea**. That is to say, limit your essay topic mercilessly and give your readers a satisfying and interesting reading experience. (*See pages 91–107 on composing a readable essay.*)

- **Follow the conventions of standard English usage and grammar**. Use your computer's spell-checker and proofread your essay again and again. (*Turn to pages 143–145 on presenting a competently-written essay.*)

- **Think about your audience**. Put yourself in the shoes of your readers and ask whether anything you wrote might be unclear or ambiguous. (*See pages 113–142 for guidelines on editing your essay.*)

- **Stick to the word limit.** If a college says write between 250 and 500 words, give them them what they asked for—no fewer and no more. (*See page 144 for more on following directions.*)

- **Get feedback from others**. Let others—teachers, counselors, friends, family—read your essay and tell you in detail what your words convey about you. (*See pages 145–147 for a discussion of getting outside help.*)

Write Honestly About Yourself

Annette R, a high school senior interested in Saint Lawrence University, dealt with her stress by trying to guess what the admissions office would expect her to write in response to the charge, "Describe a significant experience or achievement that has special meaning for you." She searched the college's Web page for clues to what the college might like and found a special program called "Service Learning" that fosters good citizenship "through the development of a sense of responsibility for the welfare of others." "OK," Annette concluded, "if they like social do-gooders, I'll give them a social do-gooder." So she set out to prove that she and Saint Lawrence were meant for each other. She began her essay:

> Success depends on how well you present yourself, what you have to say and how effectively you convey your message.

> Your Web site said that Service Learning program develops a sense of responsibility for the welfare of others. I would like to attend Saint Lawrence because that description fits me perfectly. I am the type of person who likes people. I have many friends that I love dearly. I cannot walk the hallways of the high school without saying hello to someone. I am very happy that I have so many friends, and feel that I have so many because of my job. My job helps me to relate to people.

The balance of the essay described her job as a receptionist in a dentist's office, where she often comforted people in pain.

Annette had the academic credentials for Saint Lawrence, but was rejected. She had made the fatal mistake of trying to guess what she thought the college wanted, an approach always filled with peril. Admissions people don't want anything in particular except to have applicants write something that accurately portrays themselves. There are no hidden answers to the questions. Applicants "shouldn't try to figure out what a school is looking for," says Harvard/Radcliffe's admissions director Marlyn McGrath Lewis. "They should just try to convey a real and memorable sense of themselves." Lewis's words are echoed in the essay instructions from M.I.T., which say, "This application is our best attempt to learn all about you. We hope you

> Annette made the mistake of trying to guess what the college wanted.

will do your best to help us get to know you. Don't try to appear to be someone you *think* we want. Simply be yourself. We want to know you as you really are." Thus, when a college asks, "Who belongs on a modern-day Mount Rushmore?"—as William and Mary once did—there really is no "correct" answer.

In an essay about a "rewarding experience," Susan E gave Yale an honest self-portrait. She wrote about her audition for a summer school in the arts. "The tryouts," Susan said, "were not unlike writing a college essay":

> Acting is, after all, the art of revealing character, and that is what I am trying to do now: present a clear picture of Susan E's character . . . so, if you don't mind, I'm going to think of this whole affair as an audition.
>
> Actually, my experience with acting auditions is very limited. The most memorable and important audition I have ever had was for a summer theater program that I attended after my junior year. There were two auditions, a semifinal and a final round, and each time I performed two dramatic monologues. I created other people's characters and spoke other people's words. Thinking back on the experience, I believe my own character and my own words would have been infinitely more interesting. . . .

Susan then quoted the monologue she recited and describes what she felt after the audition:

> There's the tremendous feeling of accomplishment. I suppose that's a big part of it—the accomplishment. I don't imagine performing would stimulate me so much if I had no success at it. In fact, if I were lousy at it, I probably would stay clear of it as much as possible—like gym. . . . Yeah, failure generally stinks. It's very scary to fail. In fact, right about now I'm going to start the seemingly unending process of contemplating this audition. "Did it go well? Did I say too much? Was I too honest? Did I sound silly? Will they laugh about this for weeks to come?"—Paranoia strikes deep, but fear of failure strikes deeper. Then I'll go the other way: "Of course they liked you. Honesty is refreshing. It took guts to be silly and they'll respect you for it." Well, I guess I'll know soon enough.

There's more, but by now you must have noticed that there's an honest-to-goodness person writing the words here. Susan's essay could be an entry in her diary—it's that personal. It's the kind of writing that helps admissions personnel to set one applicant apart from the others. In fact, that's the whole point, says Carol A. Rowlands, director of admissions at Lafayette. "An essay should distinguish one applicant from another."

Write About Something Important to You

Colleges ask for an essay largely because they want to get to know you. When the admissions staff has finished your essay, they should have a vivid sense of your personality. If you give them only what you think they want, you're being dishonest, posing as someone you are not. An imposter may try to pass himself off in his essay as a seriously committed poet, for example. But if the rest of his application makes no reference to writing poetry, or working on publications, or taking poetry courses, readers may think twice about accepting his word. Consistency helps. Admissions officials often cite cases of students who write impassioned essays about racism, sweatshop labor, the plight of the homeless, gun laws, and other timely issues. Yet nothing in the students' records shows a particular interest in human rights, in politics, or in any current issues for that matter. Topics seem to have been pulled from the op-ed pages of newspapers.

Application essays are not meant to demonstrate your knowledge of current events. They have an altogether different purpose. As Perry Robinson, director of admissions at Denison University, says, "We want to know how well students write and whether they can address a given topic. We also hope to find out who they are, what's important to them, and why."

"Pick a topic you care about, an issue of significance and familiarity to you," says John E. Stafford, a professional guidance counselor in New York. Why? Because nothing will flop faster than an impersonal essay full of sweeping generalizations about a big issue that has puzzled experts and politicians for years. If you're going to write about the homeless, make sure you can demonstrate real knowledge and personal

> Before you write about the homeless, serve dinner in a downtown shelter.

interest. Have you, for example, served dinner in a downtown shelter, collected clothing for homeless families, or at least spoken out about the subject in your history class? Monica Barbano, a former admissions official at Muhlenberg, advises, "Write about something you feel strongly about, something you're passionate about—and not only will you be excited about it, so will we."

Andy C, applying to the University of Vermont, stumbled on a one-and-a-half page essay about global warming that began this way:

> In this day and age environmental problems are very important worldwide topics of discussion. These controversial issues have a great effect on all of society. In particular, the depletion of the ozone layer is affecting the future of mankind's habitat. In the last fifty years, the polar ice caps have receded in record amounts. . . .

Andy was probably sincere, perhaps even gravely worried, about issues surrounding global warming, but the start of his essay shows nothing personal, passionate, or especially persuasive about his concern.

Harry Bauld, a former admissions dean at Brown and Columbia, says that vague statements that go on and on about pollution, AIDS, or world hunger are called "Miss America" essays. Like beauty queens, they recite platitudes and offer simple-minded solutions to the stickiest problems. "I think the conflict between pro-life and pro-choice could be solved if both sides just sat down and had a good heart-to-heart talk," wrote one "contestant" in an application sent to Boston University.

In contrast, Inga K, applying to Johns Hopkins, laid claim to a serious interest in Finnish politics at the outset of an essay on the Finnish economy:

> Through my mother I am a Finnish citizen. She came from Finland and thought it would be a good idea for her children to hold dual citizenship. . . .
>
> Even though I am very Americanized, I still have strong ties to Finland. At home I often speak Finnish, I eat Finnish food, read Finnish magazines, and even listen to the news from Helsinki on a shortwave radio. Although I have a lot of American friends, I'm closer to the Finnish friends I have at my church. Each summer I go to Finland for about a month to visit my relatives. When I am older, I may go to there to live. I don't know yet.
>
> Lately, I have been watching closely the Finnish economy and the consequences of . . .

"The best essays," says Susan Wertheimer, dean of admissions at the University of Vermont, "come directly from the heart. Too often, students think we want to read only about 'big' themes or major life events. That's not so. One of the most memorable essays I've read was composed by a young woman who described her feelings when her best friend moved away. The topic was simple—a common experience in today's mobile culture. I understood how she felt, why the friendship had meant so much to her, how she'd coped with the loss and moved on in her life."

Write a Unique Essay—the One That Only You Can Write

Essays on topics of consuming personal interest don't always guarantee success. Sometimes you can hardly tell one from the other. They sound almost mass-produced. "We don't expect Pulitzer Prize essays," says Karen Ley, a former admissions associate at Lafayette, "just good honest efforts that tell us something about the individual writer."

When he began his essay for the Air Force Academy, Tom M didn't realize the pitfalls of assembly-line writing:

> I would like to attend the Air Force Academy because I want a good college education. I also want to learn to fly, become a military officer and serve my country.

"So do 8,000 other applicants," Tom's high school English teacher told him. "What's going to set you apart from every other candidate?" It was fortunate that Tom ran his essay through several drafts. His first effort would certainly have earned him a letter of rejection because it lacked a hook to catch the attention of an admissions official. Much later, after numerous drafts, Tom had a hook:

> "Five. Four. Three. Two. One. Blast off!"
> My friend Eric pushed the button and a red rocket, about as long as my forearm and less than half as wide, whooshed into the sky. It almost disappeared from view before we saw the opening of a small white parachute that would bring it safely back to earth. "Wow-eee," Eric and I shouted as we

> sprinted toward the landing site as fast as our eleven-year-old legs would move. Another successful launch by the founders and only members of the Linden Street Junior Birdman Club!

Tom then recalls that his love affair with flying sprouted during his days as a rocket freak in sixth grade. Although Tom finally decided not to apply to the Air Force Academy, the magnetism of his new opening paragraph would probably have stopped his folder from slipping unnoticed into the rejection pile.

Jim R, an applicant to Duke, responding to the question, "What is it you do that best reflects your personality?" devised a uniquely personal approach. He wrote a list of forty sentences, each beginning with *I*:

> I love music of every kind.
> I have never been rock-climbing, but I intend to go soon.
> I share a room with my kid brother who is a dirt-bike maniac and who often drives me up the wall.
> I hate to sit in front of people who talk in the movies.
> I grow weepy over stories of faithful dogs like Lassie and Buck.
> I could survive very well on a diet of spaghetti and Dr. Pepper.

Thirty-four sentences later, no reader could fail to recognize Jim, the person behind the essay.

When a college asks you to describe your interests, be cautious. Don't let your passion for karate, military history, or sailing distract you from the purpose of the essay—to show yourself to the college. Stay clear of the temptation to write a *World Book* article on black belts, famous battles, or boats. Matt S couldn't resist writing about the subject he loved the most. He began (and continued) in this fashion:

> One of my main interests is cartography. Some day I hope to work for the U.S. Coast and Geodetic Survey, the federal agency responsible for making and maintaining maps for the government and the public. Mapmaking is fascinating, especially because maps keep changing. Most people think that the land never changes, but with road construction, dams, floods, earthquakes, storms and fires, many maps made forty or fifty years ago are now obsolete. One of the most dramatic cartographic changes in the United States has been on Cape Cod, Massachusetts. Every decade the ocean coastline recedes

thirty feet and the bay shoreline grows a similar amount. The place where the pilgrims landed in 1620 is now a quarter of a mile offshore.

Few high school students study maps as avidly as Matt. In spite of his unusual passion, however, his essay sounds much like a geography textbook. Although a school that seeks geography majors would love this, it fails to convey the qualities that most colleges look for in application essays: ability to think on an abstract level, resilience, empathy, and a whole host of other *personal* characteristics.

Focus on a Single Area

Matt hid his personality in facts and statistics. Nevertheless, he had the good sense to focus his essay on a single topic. Not everyone does. Here, for example, is the opening of Nancy B's essay for Ohio Wesleyan:

> My four years in high school have been very rewarding and productive. As well as receiving excellent grades, I have become involved in many of the extracurricular activities offered at the school. Although at times I have been dissatisfied with some of my classes, I am generally enthusiastic about activities, and this enthusiasm has added a lot of life to the school atmosphere.
>
> In addition to academic achievements, I have developed a strong sense of leadership. This is evident in the positions I have held during the past four years as elected representative to the school government, captain of the lacrosse team, co-chair of the assemblies committee and editor-in-chief of the yearbook. . . .

Because Nancy had already listed her activities on the application, she squandered a chance to give Ohio Wesleyan more information about herself. She buried a lively personality in an essay that reads like a list of activities. Shirley Levin, an educational consultant from Rockville, Maryland, says,

Don't repeat in your essay what you've written someplace else on your application.

"It's far better to convey a feeling of pride, achievement, or accomplishment in a very small area."

Elissa G did just that in her Bryn Mawr application. Long a frustrated math student, she focused sharply on her ultimate victory over arithmetic, as this excerpt shows:

> . . . I never did get the hang of adding anything with more than one digit. I still have to think twice when multiplying six and eight. Moreover, I am completely reliant on my pencil and paper. The most annoying facet of this whole disability is that I understand and like math. Algebraic theory fascinated me, geometric proofs thrilled me and logarithms were amazing. Yet, I kept messing up tests and problems because I multiplied wrong, or added wrong or subtracted wrong . . . thank heaven for partial credit! Finally, in my sophomore year, I was rewarded for my rudimentary deficiencies. After maintaining a B average in my Trig class for a whole year, I whizzed the Regents, got a 100 and received an A in the course.

Focusing on a single area may be tough when you've done a lot with your life. By targeting one activity, though, you can show how hard you've thrown yourself into it. You can also include specific details about yourself, details that make you sound more like a real person. Consider, for example, this excerpt from Susan F's essay for Brown University:

> My most rewarding acting experience was at the Andover Summer Session. I played the ruinous young girl, Mary Tilford, in Lillian Hellman's *The Children's Hour.* The role was very different from those I was accustomed to, like the good-natured nurse, Nellie Forbush, in *South Pacific.* Mary is a sadistic, tantrum-throwing, spoiled child who can also present a most ingenuous exterior. To show her complex personality—the manipulative female, the affectionate grandchild, the nasty friend—was difficult for me. I have a tendency to repress all anger, and when Mary was alone with her peers she was vicious. In one scene I had to slap a girl who is a good friend. To make the slap believable I had to really hit her. This was almost harder than the hysterics or the cloying sweetness, but with practice was finally perfected. To my pleasure, some of the audience did take my portrayal seriously. I had several students stop me in the cafeteria and with horrified expressions exclaim, "You're so mean!" Fiction had been transformed into reality—perhaps the best review.

The Boasting Problem

Susan wanted Brown to know of her triumph on the stage. She was rightfully proud of her accomplishment, yet didn't sound boastful. Since most of us have been taught not to boast, we don't usually puff ourselves up too much. We don't want to appear conceited. Still, Shirley Levin tells college applicants, "Look, if

> **Be proud of your achievements, but don't brag.**

you don't blow your horn, nobody else will." The problem, though, is that self-impressed people rarely impress others. So, if you're good at something, tell the college, of course, but don't shout. A champion with a touch of reserve or a sense of humor is always more endearing than a braggart.

Mike M is a gifted political cartoonist, justifiably proud of his accomplishments. He injects droll humor into all his drawings. Yet in this passage from his New York University essay, which focuses on his gift, he sounds smug, maybe even arrogant:

> I would like to direct the attention of the admissions committee to my extensive involvement in political cartooning for the past four years. The responsibility of producing no less than one satirical drawing per week has necessitated my regular reading of *The New York Times* and other news publications, such as *Time* and *USA Today*. As a consequence, I have become well-informed on issues of national affairs and American foreign policy. In the future, I anticipate using my knowledge and artistic talent to raise the social consciousness of the ordinary citizen by pointing out the issues that I feel are of great importance.

Mike was accepted, but surely not for being the sort of person his essay portrays.

Similarly, a high school senior named Eliot M, evidently dazzled by his own musical achievement, didn't realize how immodest he sounded when he told Tufts:

> My extraordinary talent and accomplishments in the field of music are sufficiently noteworthy to warrant my inclusion in the highly selective all-county orchestra.

Although Eliot may deserve respect for his musicianship, he could probably use a lesson in modesty.

Actually, modesty is rather easy to learn. Just say that you consider yourself lucky to have great talent, or after telling how you've struggled to attain success, add that you're still trying to do better. For instance, Suzanne W, another exceptional musician, wrote on her Yale application:

> As a violinist, I have discovered wonderful feelings of accomplishment, surpassed only by the knowledge that it is only the beginning of a lifetime's experience.

Roger D is also blessed with excellence. He loves art and knows a lot about it. In his Columbia essay, he showed how well informed he is by relating an incident in the art museum:

> As I was standing in front of *St. Francis in Ecstasy*, two college students came over and started discussing the painting because they had to answer questions about its symbolism, composition and use of color for their art history class. Realizing that they weren't getting very far on their own, I decided to help. I pointed out religious symbolism and mentioned Giovanni Bellini's influence on Venetian painting—his use of sensuous colors and perspective. They seemed impressed by what I said, and I don't know which I enjoyed more—talking about the painting or looking at it.

The simple phrase, "I don't know," rescues Roger from sounding vain. What gave his spirits even more of a boost was that he used his knowledge to do a good turn for someone else.

Of course, excessive pride may not be your problem. Like most people, perhaps, you don't have an exceptional talent. In fact, you may be searching for something in your life that's worth writing about. Don't worry. Everyday life has been the source of many outstanding essays. In your school locker, in your work as a cashier at Target, in your close ties to a grandparent, you may find kindling for a good, sharply focused essay. For Tufts, Dave K wrote about delivering newspapers to lonely senior citizens. Every day he became an old woman's link to the world. Kenny D, applying to Michigan, described his fight against boredom as a stock clerk at a supermarket. As he unpacked boxes he became a student of shopping carts, discovering that consumers express themselves by their choice of groceries.

Dangerous Areas: Proceed with Caution

The "Jock" Essay

Although no essay topic is off limits, some contain pitfalls that you should avoid. Admissions personnel, for instance, are rarely impressed by the so-called jock essay, the one that predictably tells the reader what you learned from being first-string left tackle or playing goalie on the field hockey team. Every reasonably successful athlete has learned self-discipline, courage, and sportsmanship on the field. If a sport has truly been a crucial part of your life, your essay will have to show how. However, you'll have to do more than write the story of how winning the race made you feel, or how losing it helped to build your character.

In her application essay for the University of North Carolina, Alison L, a sprinter on the track team who suffers from exercise-induced asthma, wrote that "the word 'fun' had no place in the lexicon of track terms, while the phrase 'welcome to Hell' found itself right at home." Her essay details the agony of daily practice but then bursts with gratitude for all the benefits she derived from pushing herself to the limit:

> It is said that the strength of effort is the measure of the result, and by golly, I must have made one heck of an effort because the long-term results are wonderful and abundant. The most significant effect is the impact track has made on my health. While running, I could not conceive how the strain I was placing on my already burdened lungs could possibly improve my condition, but I soon realized that intense training expanded my lung capacity, increased my endurance, improved my muscular strength, and on top of it all, caused me to lose thirteen excess pounds.

Alison adds that track improved her performance in school, too. Before track, she procrastinated and always rushed to complete homework at the last minute. "While on the team," she wrote, "I was forced to finish assignments many days prior to the due date, in anticipation of lengthy track meets."

Brian C, a fencer, wrote a more dramatic jock essay for the University of Pennsylvania. As these excerpts show, Brian invites you into his mind during a match:

"Fencers, ready?"

"Ready, sir."

"Fence!"

. . . . I must win this bout. I have to be careful; I must find and exploit his weakness without allowing him to ensnare me with his strength. Every fencing bout starts like an argument: In the beginning, one must be patient and find out where one's opponent stands on the issue, before going in for the kill. When I was a child I would always lose arguments. Afterward I would go home and think of things I could have said to win. When I entered high school, I joined Model Congress, an organization patterned on the U.S. Congress. After three years, it has improved my verbal fencing immeasurably and I find that now I rarely lose an argument.

. . . He advances; I retreat, extend, lunge and miss. He moves in for the riposte. Panicking, I make a wild parry; he coolly disengages and I feel his point on my chest.

"Halt!" yells the director. "Touch left. Score is 3–1. Fencers ready?"

I am upset. He's scored three times as many touches on me as I have on him. If the bout continues like this, I will lose! This sport is silly; poking people with metal blades! I could be reading a book now. Reading is a wonderful pastime because every time I read I learn something new. When I read, I empathize with the characters. I feel new feelings and think new thoughts. Every book I read makes me more complete.

As he thrusts and parries, Brian also thinks about skiing, sailing, doing his physics homework, and traveling. In fewer than 500 words, Brian's personality and interests unfold. He reveals his intellect and sense of humor, his versatility, and writing skill. Because he wrote a multidimensional self-portrait, Brian has strengthened his application. After reading the essay, an admissions committee would have little difficulty deciding whether Brian belonged in their college.

Last Summer I Went to . . .

At almost any college, Brian's essay would outclass most others, especially those written on such common topics as athletics, working as a camp counselor, a wilderness adventure, and travel. Traveling, in fact, is probably the most popular subject

Travel is probably the most popular subject for college application essays.

chosen for college essays. Applicants seem extraordinarily fond of turning their travels into "significant experience" stories. Travel has virtues galore, but writing about it can be perilous. Colleges take a dim view of essays that are little more than personal narratives of "My Trip to Niagara Falls" or "What I Learned About Myself While Biking the Berkshires." The admissions offices at the University of Virginia and other colleges report that one out of every five essays seems to be about travel. Karen Ley, formerly on the admissions staff at Lafayette, remembers reading thirty accounts of summer trips in a single day. "I never knew that travel could be so tedious," she says.

Once in a while, though, someone writes a gem of a travel essay, like this one that David M sent to Berkeley:

> My German teacher, Mr. Turner, has decorated his classroom with Lufthansa posters showing scenes of the Black Forest, fairy-tale castles on the Rhine and the mountains of Bavaria. There's also a beautiful sunset in Cologne, with the cathedral silhouetted against the orange sky. They are all hung there to show what we would see if we traveled to Germany, which I did last summer.
>
> In preparing for my trip I packed my 35 mm camera and a dozen rolls of color film. I wanted to be ready to take photos of all the picturesque sights we would encounter during our three-week trip. Strangely, I came back to the United States with ten rolls of film still in their boxes.

In the rest of his essay, David tells of how his attitude toward photography changed after meeting an elderly Dutchman, Mr. Gillem, in the memorial museum at Dachau, the site of a World War II concentration camp. Gillem, an art historian, talked with David at length about the uses of photography and convinced him that taking snapshots of pretty scenes merely wasted film. Pointing to photos depicting the horrors of the Holocaust, he told David to use his talent to awaken people to the wrongs of the world and to leave the scenery to postcard photographers. David closed with this paragraph:

> I took just forty pictures on my trip, mostly of people I met: Dore, a pretty girl in Hamburg, some Swiss students on the Rhine, a professor and his wife in Heidelberg and a family friend I stayed with in Karlsruhe. Also I bought about a hundred postcards and a travel poster for my German teacher. Mr. Gillem would be proud.

David's travel piece differs from most others because it focuses on an encounter with just one person. Notice, too, that the trip changed David in only a small way. He now thinks differently about taking photographs. This is a modest change and is far more credible than the grandiose claims made in countless college essays about how a summer trip transformed a student's life.

Unless you can make your travel story magical, store it in your scrapbook. Because some admissions counselors think that applicants who choose to tell about their travels are not pushing themselves creatively or intellectually, be sure you've found a fresh approach to your What-I-Did-Last-Summer essay. Don't turn an unforgettable summer adventure into a forgettable essay. For example, Tim C, an applicant to the University of Rochester, went traveling to New England and Canada, but his essay went nowhere, as this opening paragraph shows:

> An experience that has had a great meaning for me occurred the summer of my junior year. During that summer I spent a week in Maine, a week in Vermont, and a week in New Hampshire. I also visited Quebec for a briefer period of time. My trip away from home led me to mature and to obtain a better and broader picture of how other people live.

If Tim had left blank spaces where he wrote Maine, Vermont, and New Hampshire, you could fill in Maryland, Virginia, and North Carolina, or, for that matter, any other state or country on earth. The result would be the same—failure to convey the uniqueness of the experience.

Any essay that offers a stock response to a question is what Harry Bauld, a longtime reader of application essays, calls "the noose with which a seventeen-year-old can hang himself." In effect, such essays can work against you in the admissions office. Margaret Drugovich, in charge of admissions at Ohio Wesleyan, concurs. "Unique presentations are a welcome break from bundles of monotonous, repetitive essays," she observes, "and then almost always work to the student's advantage." To ensure that your essay will stand out, choose your topic with great care, particularly if you are inclined to write about travel or any other of the most popular topics, such as sports, family, friends, and the agony of writing an application essay.

Don't turn an unforgettable summer adventure into a forgettable essay.

AN ESSAY THAT WORKS 25

Answering the Offbeat Question

Many colleges, hoping to draw out the uniqueness of an applicant's personality, make unusual requests on their applications, some of them downright wacky. The University of Chicago asks you to describe a picture and explore "what it wants." Carleton wants you to write about an "important question you wish we had asked." The admissions office at William and Mary wants to know whether you'd return to your hometown to begin your adult life after graduation. And Stanford University instructs you to write a 10-line note to your future roommate relating a personal experience that reveals something about you.

Such questions aren't meant to stump or trick you. It doesn't matter to the folks in the Chicago admissions office whether your picture is a photo, a painting, or a cartoon. They just want to know you better and see if you can think and write. When Johns Hopkins asks you to tell them how you would spend a full day when you had no homework, no responsibilities, and no commitments, they are not merely checking your interests and values. They want to know *why* you'd be driven to build a birdhouse rather than, say, hang out on MySpace or hike in the mountains with your portable MP3 player for company.

An offbeat question doesn't obligate you to write an offbeat answer. Essays that seem to have been written mainly to shock the reader or attract attention "are generally off-putting and tend to hide rather than showcase a candidate's special qualities," according to William M. Shain, dean of admissions at Bowdoin. If you are naturally creative, write a creative essay, but if creativity is not your strong suit, write factually about your beliefs and feelings. You'll never be penalized for being honest and straightforward. "Above all," adds Shain, "avoid gimmicks. They almost never improve an essay." The high school quarterback who wrote his Columbia essay on a football did little to enhance his chances of being admitted. Nor did an Ohio Wesleyan applicant who for no apparent reason mailed in an essay attached to a coconut.

If faced with an oddball question, beware of being too cute in your response. Some years ago, when Stanford asked, "What adjective do you think would be most frequently used to describe you by those who know you best?" one jokester replied, "terse," and

> Beware of being too cute. If creativity isn't your strong suit, just be honest and straightforward.

didn't write the essay. University officials were not amused. In contrast, they were charmed by Elissa G's answer:

> It's a nice little word—"intriguing." It carries that suave nuance of smoky cafes and *Casablanca* or a James Bond movie. All of which are not exactly appropriate, since I could never imagine myself in a sleek, black evening gown, picking up a tall handsome guy in a wild, Latin nightclub only to have my romance completely spoiled by my father's kidnapping, etc. How boring. I'm not knocking the connotation though. I rather like being a dark and mysterious lady.
>
> Yet "intriguing" is just a bit more than a connotation. It's the ability to interest people and to keep them interested. It's a slightly contagious enthusiasm that interests people—that attracts them to you, your ideas, or your activities. That is something I certainly can do. For I can help triple the size of the Debate Team, or try something new with the yearbook, or surprise a close friend with an innovative idea . . . . and with any luck, I can intrigue you.

In her first paragraph Elissa toys with the meaning of her word, but in the second she reveals its substance. Any admissions official would be "intrigued" by Elissa and want to know more about her.

Answering the Ordinary Question

An oddball essay question may inspire quirky answers but an ordinary question shouldn't tempt you to write an ordinary response. A typical question may ask, "What personal or academic experiences were particularly rewarding for you—a project, teacher, piece of writing or research, a particular course of study?" Although the question suggests that you write about school, you are free to pick any experience whatever. You may be better off, in fact, if you choose a unique personal experience. Finding your own topic demonstrates your initiative. You can also bet that most other people will play it safe and write about school. Don't run with the crowd—unless

Take the less-traveled route; choose a topic that's distinctly yours.

you know that you can beat them. Otherwise, take the less-traveled route. Choose a topic that is distinctly yours. (See Chapter 3 for lots of suggestions.)

Because unusual creativity is not essential, you can bring out your best in a sober, sensitive, and sincere essay as well. Just don't get caught in the trap of dry, long-winded and empty prose, like the writer who began his self-appraisal this way:

> During one's four years in secondary school, one's education is centered around a number of different things that hopefully will be helpful in college and in the career one pursues.

Yes, the point may be understandable, but the writing is dull and impersonal. Compare it to a more provocative statement like this:

> This whole college admission business is downright crazy. Very little of it has to do with education itself, and more with meeting deadlines, following procedures, and taking tests. So far, my image of college is a place dominated by rules and regulations and sorting students into categories according to some numeric scale. It makes me wonder if all that I learned in high school classes was a waste of time and effort. I sure hope not, but applying to college has prepared me to be disappointed.

At least you hear a person's voice in those words, and that's what colleges listen for.

College admissions people generally agree that the worst essays are those that summarize the writer's high school career. Nevertheless, students keep pumping out boring recitals of what they did since ninth grade. Such writers miss an opportunity to tell the college something distinctive about themselves. Their responses also suggest an inability to think deeply and to develop ideas about a single topic. Even worse, they reveal an unwillingness to take an intellectual risk, to extend themselves beyond the ordinary and mundane. Aiming to please, they submit safe, dull essays that invariably fall flat in the admissions office.

Hoping to inspire more potent writing, Connecticut College encourages applicants to "enjoy the experience." In fact, they say that they "look forward to reading your work and getting to know you a little bit better." Oberlin declares, "Don't be afraid to take a risk, to be original, to tell us about successful or not-so-successful experiences." Similarly, applicants to the University of Chicago are told to address topics "with utter seriousness, complete fancy, or something in between." Further instructions say, "Play, analyze (don't agonize), create, compose—let us hear the result of your thinking about something that interests you, in a voice that is your own."

Humor in Your Essay

Although essays that contain gimmicks, like puns, coined words, slang, and fractured English, may attract attention among thousands of ordinary essays, your attempt to be clever may tarnish your application. An ill-timed wisecrack could miss the funny bone of a weary admissions dean. This doesn't mean you should avoid humor. On the contrary: since you have plenty of opportunity to be sober and serious in the rest of the application, in the essay you can give your wit a workout. Readers will relish something playful, satirical, or whimsical. Don't overdo it, though. Tread lightly and cautiously with jokes and sarcasm. What you and your friends may think is uproarious in the school lunchroom could fall on its face in the admissions office. In an essay submitted to Northwestern, a student joked that he would kill himself if he was rejected. "That wasn't funny," said a staffer in the admissions office. "The applicant didn't understand the concept of boundaries—of what is and isn't acceptable." Therefore, test your humor on an impartial adult before you send it to a college. If you're not usually a funny person, don't try to become one on your application. David Lettermans are not made overnight.

> In your essay you can give your wit a workout.

Sometimes gentle, self-effacing humor is best. No one at Harvard, for example, objected to Lisa E's tongue-in-cheek account of why she no longer dreamed of becoming an Amazon explorer:

> I would not make a very good adventurer for two reasons: motion sickness and ignorance. I am particularly prone to seasickness—an unfortunate circumstance, since the proper way for adventurers to travel is in boats, preferably shipwrecked ones. As for ignorance, I am prone to ignorance in all areas; although in this case I am referring only to my ignorance of jungle survival tactics. I would undoubtedly perish within twenty-four hours of my arrival in the Amazon by drowning in a bog, treading on a sleeping snake, or ingesting a poiso-

nous species of mushroom or grub. Then again, I might be stricken by some dread jungle malady or consumed for brunch by the very tribe of cannibals I had intended to study. Even worse, I might finally arrive in the Amazon only to find myself accosted by vendors of tribal nose rings and "I survived the Amazon" tee shirts.

In writing about a significant experience for the University of Pennsylvania, Joel B poked fun at his own ineptness as an outfielder in a childhood baseball game:

The game begins. Joel stolidly assumes his usual position in right field. Anxiety dominates his emotions. He is forced to stand outside on a field on a hot and sticky day, surrounded by clouds of swarming gnats. He fears that a ball may never be hit to him, and the only thing more fearful than that would be for a ball to be hit to him. His pet peeve on the baseball diamond is the "easy" pop fly. Joel wishes that people wouldn't include the word easy every time that phrase is used. He could be back in school demonstrating his academic prowess. Yes, school is a place where little Joel could shine! No one could hold a candle to his mastery of multiplication tables. Not to mention spelling. *There* is a field in which he could compete with the best of them.

In Sabrina E's essay for the University of Chicago you also find humor, but humor with a bite:

Before I arrived in my present high school, I attended school in Ireland. There are many differences between American and Irish education, not the least of which is the priority placed on actual teaching. Though in America scholarship comes first, in Ireland more time is spent trying to keep us on the paths of virtue than in steering us toward the paths of wisdom. Indeed, it seemed that a veritable legion of nuns was employed solely to safeguard our morals.

Whenever one of our regular teachers was absent, we were treated to one of Sister Assumpta's lectures. This latter-day saint was, by her own account, in direct communication with God. Apparently, each night as she prepared for bed, she would fall into a trance and converse with Him. This meant that whatever she told us came directly from the horse's mouth, although we were more inclined to believe that it came from the opposite end of the same animal.

Knowing that her irreverence might disqualify her at some colleges, Sabrina sent the essay anyway. She took a gamble, but for her it was worth it, since she wouldn't have wanted to attend a college where her humor wasn't appreciated.

Whether the application questions are cute, common, or challenging, all colleges have the same basic reason for asking applicants for one or more pieces of writing. As the Columbia application puts it, "Write an essay which conveys to the reader a sense of who you are." Jennifer Stein, Associate Director of Admissions at Connecticut College, says it another way: "The essay serves as a mechanism for getting a glimpse at the human being behind the numbers."

As you begin to think about how you'll present yourself as a person to the college of your choice, keep asking two key questions: What's unique about me, and what do I want my reader to think of me? In your answers you're sure to find the seed of an essay that will work.

Reading Your Essay

Like customers, readers are always right. Maybe you won't like what they think about your essay. Maybe they'll misunderstand your intentions. They're still right. They get what they get—it's that simple.

Even the best writers can't always predict how readers will respond to their work. That's why you should plan to show your application essay to an unbiased reader or two before you submit it to a college. Ask your readers to tell you their impressions of the writer. If their impressions coincide with what you've intended, you're likely to have written a successful essay. Connecticut College's Jennifer Stein urges students to "remember that a human being is reading their essays, not a nameless, faceless 'Board of Admissions.' Write for someone—a friend, a family member, a teacher," Stein advises, "and your essay will be more personal and interesting."

In the pages that follow you'll be privy to thoughts and reactions of a college admissions officer recorded alongside the text of four essays. Then, you'll see the final evaluation of each candidate's work.

(*Note*: Because admissions officials often find themselves inundated with piles of applications, they typically respond to essays with a few marginal notes and a brief summary statement. For the following essays, however, comments are spelled out in greater detail to better illustrate matters that essay readers think about as they evaluate applicants' essays.)

Joyce B

If someone were to ask me to describe myself, I would have to say that I am a person of many interests. I enjoy a simple life, yet I am not afraid to try new things.

> Fairly dull opening. Hope it gets better. Essay has three parts: many interests, simple life, and new things. One topic, in depth, would probably be better.

I have been fortunate enough to become exposed to a variety of life-styles at a very early age. During my travels to Europe I was able to visit Germany, Italy, and Switzerland. There, I learned about different cultures and how other people live. Watching and meeting people is one of the many things that I enjoy.

> "exposed"? Did she live the lifestyles or just observe them? "early age"? Three? Four? Ten? I wonder what she means. What could she have learned at age three?

Since the age of four, I have been dancing with "Dance Capri," a countywide Italian-American folk-dancing group. My involvement in this organization has introduced me to people who are interested in some of the same things I am. We enjoy learning about our Italian heritage and pride ourselves in keeping up the folk-dancing tradition.

> No more travels? Now she's into dancing. How often does she dance? A major pastime?

> Ah! She likes to join groups. That's good. I wonder if she speaks Italian.

Along with dancing, traveling, and meeting new people, I enjoy skiing and gymnastics. I usually ski in Vermont during my vacations, but last year I had the opportunity to ski in Quebec, Canada, for a week. I have always been on gymnastics teams, during the school year and the summer, and although I never won any special honors, I enjoy competitive gymnastics meets, especially the balance beam. For me, competing with a team has taught me what working for one common cause and reaching one common goal are like.

> Good transition. But she's switched her focus again!

> Not another topic! Athletics. Well, we can use her on the gymnastics team.

> Not much new here. Pretty trite. An example could make this sound more honest.

One of the most relaxing hobbies I enjoy is cooking. When time permits, I bake and I prepare special meals for my family. I learned how to cook through various cooking courses that I took when I was younger. In high school, I could only fit one food preparation class into my program.

Why were the courses special? Good grades? She seems diligent. I bet her teachers and counselors say she's a plugger.

She's been busy, all right. How much time could she have given to these jobs? I better check her list of work experiences.

Along with this class, I enjoyed a variety of other courses in high school. However, the ones I liked the most were jewelry, Italian and history. I believe, though, that I made the most out of every course I took in high school.

Out of school, I invest a good deal of time in various part-time jobs. My work experience includes cashier and hostess work in an Italian restaurant, and my present job, which is working as a Gal Friday in an insurance office. I also baby-sit when I have the time.

What values?

Upbeat ending. But "youth faces tomorrow" isn't too interesting.

High school was and still is a time of growing and maturing for me. Although working hard and getting good grades has always been my first priority, I also established and set many of the values that guide my life today. I can confidently say that in my senior year of high school I am ready to meet the challenges of college. I am ready to move on, and I see a bright future ahead of me.

Note to Admissions Committee:

Joyce B's essay suggests an active, but fragmented life. Joyce skids breezily from topic to topic, to topic, suggesting just casual involvement in many areas. Yes, she's well rounded, but so are most of our applicants. I can't find anything to distinguish her from others. After reading her essay, I don't know her very well.

Her writing is essentially correct, but it's boring. Not one of her paragraphs is developed beyond presenting some general facts about herself. Too much of her essay reiterates information already stated in her application. Moreover, Joyce fails to deliver what she promises in her opening passage. Where, for one, is her "simple life?" I recommend "rejection" unless there's evidence in her file that contradicts my impression.

Chandra B

This is the fourth essay I'm writing, and it won't be any easier than any of the first three. You see, it isn't that I enjoy writing these essays, but with each one I have found out a little bit more about myself, and that is important to me. The purpose of each essay, of course, is to show that I have a sense of who I am, but there is always more to be found at the bottom of the well called "me." I wouldn't be fooling you or anyone if I said I know absolutely, totally everything there is to know about me.

My mother said to me this evening, as she finished reading my third essay, "You know what theme I find recurrent in each of these, Chandra? A sense of struggle, of some sort of tension within you. And that, I think, is what drives you. It is helping you in your maturation. Perhaps it needs resolving, but at the same time you know it is there, and you are dealing with it."

I think that for everyone sooner or later there is a time of inner tension and struggle—a time when one asks, "Who am I? What do I mean to myself?" It is those who face this struggle and deal with it rather than deny it, who eventually succeed in being who they want to be. One must learn to make choices about what one wants to stand for, to do with one's life, and at the same time one must learn to change oneself in order to achieve this.

My first essay dealt with a struggle in choosing between a German heritage and a Jewish one. My choice, however, was neither one nor the other, but a compromise to accept both as being part of me, to reconcile rather than to deny. My second essay dealt with a choice I may still have to make, namely between choosing marine biology or genetics as a career. This is a choice I may never have to make, for I may discover something I want to do more than either of them. I have not limited myself to only these two choices. Yet even now, I think I would decide upon marine biology, not because I find it more interesting, for I find

Hmmm, a common topic—the struggle of writing an essay.

Well, this is different: The struggle has been worth it. She's learned about herself. I wonder what she's learned?

Perceptive. A good idea! We can't know ourselves completely, can we?

Hmm, a sensitive mother, but c'mon, no mother talks like that. She sounds like a psychology text. Good point, though, and the dialogue adds life.

Vague paragraph. A bit ponderous. I wonder what she's driving at.

Now I see! She's been struggling for an identity. And it hasn't been easy. Her mother was right.

Struggle to communicate? That's splendid! Chandra's a deep thinker.

them both equally so, but because I enjoy it more; I have more fun with it. My third essay dealt with a struggle I will always face, namely my need to communicate. I feel the need to know about others, and to have others learn about me. This is my way of sharing myself and partaking in others. My struggle is a fight against misunderstanding and loneliness. When we communicate, whether between people or nations, we understand each other. When we communicate, we bridge the gap of loneliness.

She seems highstrung, a little tense. Is that why she's lonely? I wonder what her teachers say.

Ah, she's come back to the struggle again. Conclusion recalls her opening. Nice way to unify the piece.

There will always be struggles within me, dilemmas I will face. I am determined to resolve these tensions. With each choice, I choose who I am, who I will become. Most importantly, though, it is I who makes these choices, not someone else. That is what self-determination is all about.

She's convinced me. I believe she'll win her struggle. Strong, up-beat ending.

Note to Admissions Committee:

Chandra B views life as a serious undertaking. Her writing has conviction. She's not going to play her way through college or engage in foolishness. Her thoughtful—nay, philosophical—ideas attest to her maturity. She probably drives herself hard, maybe compulsively. She seems genuinely bound on a quest to find an identity.

Will she study hard in college? You bet, and will probably get A's. Will she contribute to the college? Intellectually, yes, and maybe in other ways, too. Let's accept her and several more passionate thinkers like her. I hope that her teacher and counselor recommendations confirm my impression that Chandra is a rare find.

Angela C

As far back as I can remember, I have excelled at sports. I was always the first in my kindergarten class to reach the swings during recess and the first to climb to the top of the rope during gym. However, while most six-year-old girl athletes tend to develop into "school-yard jocks," I seemed to lack that aggressive, competitive nature. I was much more content reading my book than keeping up with the boys. By the time I entered high school, I was clearly defined as a "student," not a "jock."

When I tried out for the field hockey team in ninth grade, it was merely because a good friend of mine begged me to do it with her. The idea of spending three hours every day running around a field didn't particularly appeal to me, but for a friend I'd do anything. After two weeks, my friend quit. Quitting has always been anathema to me, but in this case it never entered my mind anyway. I was having fun. Those three hours of practice were the best part of my day. I loved being outside, and being physically active. Most importantly, I loved being with my teammates. Between studying and practicing the piano, I'd spend so much time alone that my time on the field became a welcome and necessary break in my day. Also, coming home at six o'clock every evening helped me to budget my time, since I knew I only had a few hours in which to complete my assignments.

It wasn't until my sophomore year that field hockey became more important to me than just a social activity. It was still terrific fun since I loved getting to know the juniors and seniors on the team whom otherwise I would never have met. Some of them are still my closest friends. However, playing on the varsity squad was a very different experience from playing on the freshman team. I found myself missing holidays and giving up weekends to play hockey. The team now required a serious dedication and commitment, which I was willing to make since I enjoyed it so much. As my commitment became more serious, so did my attitude toward field hockey. I realized that I couldn't accept being a mediocre player.

Starts off like another "jock" essay—but very graceful. An appealing opening.

Oh, she's not a jock, after all. Smooth shift from kindergarten to ninth grade.

Well, she's a student and an athlete.

A rich paragraph! Shows Angela's loyalty to friends. Her perseverance, too. And the fun she's had.

And she has other interests, too.

She's well organized. That shows in her essay.

Good transition. This is moving right along. Angela is a serious hockey player.

She's obviously committed to the sport. Good, detailed writing.

She's a hard driver, too.

Interesting! She took on a challenge and won, and she's proud of her achievement. A good point.

Effective conclusion. She's summarizing her career and showing how she's changed.
Good writing. How successful she's been! And modest, too.

What determination! I think she'll make it. She's unstoppable.

Mediocre is one of the most negative words I know. I knew in my sophomore year that, as the new player on the varsity team, I was also an average player. Traveling to Holland with my field hockey team revealed to me again my inadequacies when I saw the skill of some of the Europeans. Since then, by attending camps and clinics and playing in summer leagues, I've really worked hard to become a good player. I always want to be good—if not the best—at everything to which I set my mind. To be a good student comes naturally to me, but for me to be a good field hockey player requires work.

I remember when I first started playing field hockey. I thought that to be an all-county player and captain of the varsity was to be the best. Well, I *am* an all-county player and I *am* the captain of the team but one thing I am certainly not, is the best. Whenever I achieve one of my many goals, it always seems as if a new one appears ahead of me. Now that I'm a good high school player, I'm ready to start at the bottom again and work to become a good college player.

Note to Admissions Committee:

Angela C clearly demonstrates self-confidence and an upbeat personality. She's good at everything, and she enjoys all she does. Her essay indicates that she's loyal, well-organized, determined, committed to success, industrious, and fun-loving. Yet, she doesn't bowl you over with her attributes. Instead, she casually tosses them into the story of her growth as a field hockey player. In spite of all her virtues, she neither brags nor sounds like a Boy Scout. She's an all-round scholar-athlete.

Angela can write! There's not an ill-chosen word or awkward phrase in the piece. Could she have received help? Look for confirmation of writing talent in her grades and references.

My recommendation: If she's really as good as she sounds, offer her the dean's house and a Ferrari!

Eric H

It is Friday afternoon, a time I can so vividly remember enjoying. School would let out, and no matter how much homework I had, I could always relax Friday and Saturday. Unfortunately, T.G.I.F. has evolved into O.S.I.F. (Oh @#$%, it's Friday!).

Joint custody: an American revolution. Friday is the transition day, the day that a week's worth of subsistence materials have to be transported from one parent's abode to the other's. My room at Dad's has to be cleaned, my clothes washed and pressed, and other essentials placed in order. Then my odyssey commences. Somehow, I have to get all of my belongings from one end of town to the other.

Usually, Mom picks me up. She tries to be tolerant but at times loses her cool. "I'm only going to do this once. If you forget anything, that's your tough luck." I try to explain that I can't fit everything I own into her Toyota. Sometimes she forgets that I didn't ask for this asinine way of life. In any event, four trips to the car later, we leave home and head for home.

By the time I'm really settled, another week has passed. O.S.I.F.!, and I find myself out of breath exactly where I started. In the span of two weeks I have accomplished nothing except total aggravation. I can't even blink for fear that another Friday will come.

Like anything else, joint custody has its bright side. When my parents were divorced, Dad had a big decision to make: pack up and forget his little brats or remain for the duration. Even though he's never been nominated for any Best Daddy awards, he hasn't regretted his decision to stay.

The entire ordeal has brought us a world closer. When we were quite suddenly hurled into an unamiable apartment without Mom, we shared a common interest: survival. Neither of us knew how to break an egg, sew a hem, or clean a toilet bowl.

He refused to learn these things, so I had to. Today, six years later, I cook all the meals, do all the shopping, and make most of the household decisions in place of my father. He basically grants me a generous expense account of forty dollars on Friday night,

---

A catchy opening.

Oh, another essay on divorce.

"subsistence materials" Ugh! Does he mean toothpaste, underwear, a week's supply of socks?"

"abode," "commences" Too fancy.

Mother sounds like an ogre, probably the villain in this story.

"asinine" Good word. Eric sounds bitter.

Ah, a good line. Sardonic humor.

I don't get the point of all this. Does he mean that his life is a treadmill? Why doesn't he say so?

Ah, good. There's a bright side to the story.

Well, Dad's no hero either.

Shows maturity and responsibility, I guess.

Forty dollars? Only forty dollars? that's hard to swallow!

Puzzling. Didn't he grow close to his father? Something's missing here.

and it is up to me to see that food is purchased for the week. This burden has done wonders for my character. Many of my friends fear life at college, but not I. If I can tolerate life with my father, campus life will undoubtedly be a breeze.

Another advantage to joint custody is variety. Just when I get sick of the accumulated dishes, dirty laundry, and ravenous cockroaches that are a way of life at my Dad's, I can run to Mom's for a week. Come the next Friday, you can be sure that I'll be so fed up with my mother's vexatious organization and fetish for punctuality that I'll welcome cockroaches with open arms. I think that's what is meant by escapism.

Well, good. He can make jokes, despite his misery.

It has been suggested that I stop writing essays complaining about joint custody and simply leave half of my stuff at either house. It seems logical. Maybe that's the problem; it makes sense. I don't think divorce and custody were destined by the Almighty to make sense. I suppose I just have some psychological aversion to leaving fifty percent of my life unattended for a week.

Who suggested?

Well stated

All in all, I suppose joint custody isn't so bad. I'm never bored, and I'm always on my toes. Oh @#$%, I've got to run. It's Friday!

Cute ending.

Note to Admissions Committee:

Eric H certainly has courage! He took a personal gamble by writing about an obviously painful subject. It's not that he's looking for sympathy, but rather he chose to vent his anger about being shuttled between his parents each week. He has a right to be bitter, but I question his judgment in using the application essay as a place to blow off steam.

The essay is meant to be humorous, and it is—to a point. The humor is a thin disguise, though, for someone who laughs to hide his tears. My guess is that Eric's anguish makes him hard to like, but I'd like to know what his counselor and teachers think.

He's not a bad writer, but he seems to flaunt his vocabulary—not always successfully—perhaps thinking that college people will be impressed. His work lacks polish, but I think that in time it will improve.

His essay works neither for nor against his candidacy. My recommendation will be based on the other information in his application and file.

3 WHAT TO WRITE ABOUT

Writing an essay may be a super pain to you, but colleges look at it differently. They view it as an opportunity—a chance for you to add vital information to your application about your experiences, talents, character, personal philosophy, and zest for living. In short, colleges are offering you an opportunity to convince them that you are too good to turn down.

Instructions on the University of North Carolina application put it this way:

> Because we can't meet all of our applicants personally, please help us get to know you better through the following essays. Feel free to be as serious or as humorous as you'd like; feel free also to write about something other than yourself if you feel that, by doing so, you'll help us gain a better understanding of who you are and how you think.

All colleges don't try as hard as UNC to urge applicants to be themselves in their essays, but they all want the same thing—for you to portray yourself in writing—and they give you one or more questions, or "prompts," to get you started.

Colleges and universities have devised hundreds of different prompts. Some offer a choice, others tell you to write whatever you please, as though to test your creativity. Still others lay out strict essay guidelines, partly to see whether you can follow directions. Several colleges ask for a response to a single question, then give you the option of writing a second essay on another topic—an option you definitely should take if you're serious about attending that college.

Common Application Questions

Many questions that colleges ask are strikingly like those found on the Common Application. In fact, because the list of colleges using the Common Application grows every year, don't be surprised to find yourself responding to one of the "Commonapp" questions. (In

2008, over a million essays were submitted to the 300-plus colleges and universities using the Common Application.)

Responses to these questions frequently overlap. If you were to write on a significant experience (the most popular topic), for example, you might tell a story about an influential person in your life (another favorite). Or your significant experience might have led you to develop a serious interest in an issue of national or global concern, and so on.

But even if you don't actually fill out a Common Application, odds are high that you'll write on a topic that resembles one of the six prompts found in the essay section of the Commonapp.

The "Significant Experience" Question

> Evaluate a significant experience, achievement, risk you have taken, or ethical dilemma you have faced and its impact on you.

So you haven't won a lottery, performed on American Idol, or ridden your bike across the country. Nor have you totalled your family car or been mugged. In other words, you've lived a pretty ordinary life and feel as though you don't have a super-significant experience to write about. If that describes you, take heart, because it's possible to write a winning "significant experience" essay even though you've never made headlines.

Here's why: *Significant experience* is a relative term. An experience is "significant" if you make it so. It need not be significant to anyone else, but it could be a dynamite topic anyway if the experience was significant to you. In responding to the question, then, your job is to identify an experience and show its impact on you.

One of the best essays sent recently to the University of Vermont was composed by an applicant who described her emotions when her best friend moved away. Although that is a common experience in today's mobile society, she wrote it directly from her heart. She made clear how she felt, why the friendship had meant so much to her, and how she had coped with the loss and moved on in her life.

Notice that the prompt also defines a significant experience as an *achievement, a risk you have taken, or an ethical dilemma*, categories that open up many possibilities for an essay. Again, your achievement, risk, or dilemma need not be earth-shaking or even newsworthy. But it merits an essay if it was significant to you in some way.

In choosing a topic, be aware of the following do's and don'ts:

DO . . .

   ✓ Write an essay that directly addresses the prompt.

   ✓ Write about something significant that really happened to you, rather than something you heard or read about.

   ✓ Try to pick a specific experience or event that left a positive rather than a negative impact on you.

   ✓ Choose a fairly recent experience or event, one that you remember clearly (colleges want to know you as you are today, not the way you used to be).

   ✓ If you write about taking a risk, be sure to contrast what you hoped to gain with the consequences of failure.

DON'T . . .

   ✗ Devote most of your essay to telling about the experience. Rather, focus on what the experience has meant to you or what you learned from it.

   ✗ Hesitate to dramatize your experience using dialogue and other story-writing techniques.

   ✗ Choose an X-rated experience (colleges don't need to know *everything* about you).

   If you write about a dilemma, don't pick one that lacks an ethical dimension—for instance, whether to take the SAT or the ACT. Much better: Whether to report cheating on a final exam.

Excerpts from Answers That Worked

CONNIE G

Last year, my grandmother, "Ya-ya," fell and broke her hip. With no one to turn to because my parents were away on a business trip, I acted fast. I dialed 911, checked Ya-ya into the hospital, filled out all the forms, dealt with the doctors and nurses in the ER, OK'ed the necessary surgery, and spent the night at Ya-ya's bedside. Only then did I phone my parents.

. . . That day marks my transformation from a child to an adult. From then on, I knew that I had it in me to handle almost any difficult situation.

KINCAID R

Picking a quotation to put under my yearbook picture has been one of the hardest but ultimately most satisfying experiences I had in high school. I searched for a quote to represent me fully and truthfully, and in the process I rejected hundreds of sayings, lines from famous poems, song lyrics, slogans, and proverbs. Most of them seemed like recycled cheese, or too sappy or ill-fitting. When I finally narrowed my choices to ten, that's when the fun began. I had to analyze each quote in light of my concept of myself, and as I studied each one I began to understand who I am, who I am not, who I pretended to be but never could be, and who I aspire to become. That is to say, I examined myself more closely and thoughtfully than ever before and came to an eye-opening conclusion . . . .

By now, I'll bet you're dying to know which quotation I finally chose but I'm reluctant to tell you. I want to be accepted in college based not on what I think of myself but on what you think of my record, my achievements, and my potential to be an asset to your institution.

NIKKI T

During my first year volunteering at the Speech and Language Development Center for children with speech problems and other disabilities, I met Joseph, a vivacious, sometimes vicious, six-year old who pulled other children's hair, hid in closets and cabinets, threw his teachers' belongings on the floor, and laughed wickedly almost the whole day through.

On my first day I was given the task of disciplining Joseph, a job I embraced because I love challenges and knew it would help others. After observing Joseph for two hours I contemplated my options. I could keep him inside at recess, but since he was learning disabled, I figured he didn't understand that his actions were inappropriate. He would probably grow angry and cause even more trouble. With this in mind, I chose a second option. I took Joseph outside, sat with him on the swings and gently began to talk with him. Eventually I got around to explaining why it wasn't right to deliberately annoy other people. I gave him an example I hoped he would understand: Winnie the Pooh, I told him, would never pull Eeyore's tail off, so he, Joseph, shouldn't tug at other kids' hair. Suddenly, his eyes lit up. I knew at that moment he understood what I meant.

. . . As months went by, I was amazed and thrilled whenever I saw Joseph. He gradually turned into a completely different kid. His teachers said he was now their model student. I like to think that I made the right decision on that first day and helped make a difference in his behavior. Because of my success with Joseph, I am tending toward a teaching career, possibly as a specialist in learning disabilities.

WILHELMINA R

Last year in American History I had the honor of being chosen as co-editor of a class publication on colonial America to be modeled on *American Heritage* magazine. For many months we toiled. At times my position did not seem like an honor at all, but a punishment. Nothing would come together. I argued with my co-editor about what to do. Then I wrote an article on the French and Indian War that served as a catalyst. In short order, classmates started making trips to the library, talking with teachers, instant messaging with friends in other schools, frantically searching the Internet for interesting material for articles of their own.

. . . Through all this, I edited my classmates' work, helping simple drafts blossom into masterpieces. I suddenly realized that the articles needed bibliographies or lists of works consulted or cited. I sat down immediately and wrote a guide called "How to Cite Sources" for the class. The teacher said it was perfect and would become a permanent text for her future classes.

. . . A tremendous amount of work went into the publication. I am very, very proud of our class for accomplishing that, not only because we did an excellent piece of work but because we did it as a team. After a rocky start, our team developed creative solutions to tough new problems and put all individual differences aside to pull together. It was extremely rewarding to fly over the hurdles together. Our class gave the group performance of our lives—truly a moment of school life at its best.

The "Important Issue" Question

Discuss some issue of personal, local, national, or international concern and its importance to you.

It shouldn't be difficult to find an issue that's personally important to you. Because everyone has problems and concerns, the possibilities are literally endless—from the everyday worries of college applicants everywhere (Which teachers should I ask for a recommendation? What if my college roommate is a slob?) to idiosyncratic interests that show your individuality (ferris wheel safety; the need to reduce global light pollution). Any number of issues related to you or to your circle of friends, family, and acquaintances can be turned into gripping essays. No topic is necessarily off limits, provided that it's presented tastefully—but if a personal issue is very private, you may not want to air it in an application essay. One applicant recently sent an essay to Stanford about date rape. She described it in vivid, even graphic, terms. The admissions committee was stunned; they thought the essay crossed the line, and the applicant was wait-listed.

An essay on a local, national, or international issue requires a different approach. While there's nothing wrong with an essay on global warming, abortion, capital punishment, gun control, or war, these are topics likely to be chosen by many other applicants. If you're bursting with opinions on any of these or a similar issue, that's fine, but make sure your essay shows why you are particularly and personally concerned about it. Be prepared to discuss your point of view and to back up your opinions with convincing evidence.

DO . . .

✓ Pick an issue that has a direct effect on you.

✓ Provide evidence showing that you've been actively concerned about the issue for some time.

✓ Include fresh and original insights about the issue.

✓ Avoid writing a textbook summary of a local, national, or international concern.

DON'T . . .

✗ Choose a issue that many other applicants are likely to write about.

✗ Choose a local, national, or international issue that you couldn't have cared less about until now.

✗ Forget to focus on *your* concerns, not the concerns of editorial writers, parents, teachers, TV's talking heads, etc.

✗ Be reluctant to take an unpopular position— provided you can back up your views with a compelling rationale.

Excerpts from Answers That Worked

KRISTIN B

Last year, when my grandfather had a stroke and was dying of cancer in the hospital, I participated in a family decision to remove life support to let him die peacefully and end his suffering. At first, I thought it was a horrible and wrong thing to do.

Then Maggie, a nurse in the hospital, gave me an essay by Sidney Hook after I talked with her at length about my grandfather. The essay, "In Defense of Voluntary Euthanasia," supports a pro-euthanasia opinion. At one point in his life Hook had a near-death experience and includes it in his essay, giving the essay a realistic and personal effect. "I have already paid my dues to death—indeed, although time has softened my memories, they are vivid enough to justify my saying that I suffered enough to warrant dying several times over. Why run the risk of more?" Hook felt like he had his fill of happiness in life and therefore he had no need to prolong it. In addition, he felt that procedures that are used to prolong lives but don't lead to recovery are terrible and costly inconveniences to the patient's family members.

I'm glad Maggie showed me the essay. It changed my mind. It made the terrible decision more acceptable to me. . . .

FLOYD I

In his article "Breaking the Silence," which I read in Social Studies class, Pete Hamill ascribes problems of urban blacks to members of the black middle class. Basically, he says that middle-class blacks have abandoned their lower-class brothers by fleeing the inner city, going to college, and getting decent jobs. While the article pertains to poor, urban blacks, the issue exists in my mostly-white suburban high school, too. . . .

There are just a a handful of blacks in AP courses, for example. Most of them hang out with each other and with white kids. They have little to do with the vast majority of other black students, who have segregated themselves into remedial classes and have claimed certain corners of the school grounds as their turf. Simply walking through the hallways, an observer can easily tell which areas are considered "black" and which are considered "white." Of course there are no official rules regarding which area belongs to which group. But I know many kids who won't frequent areas because of fear of intruding, even though there is no outward animosity between blacks and whites in the school.

But rarely is there an open discussion of racial issues either. Nor is there any attempt by either group to assimilate. It seems that the two groups have decided just to go their separate ways. The administration and teachers mostly ignore the problem. Once in a while the student government raises the possibility of forming a tolerance discussion group, but they rarely draw a crowd and nothing gets accomplished.

. . . To me the situation is disheartening because schools reflect society, and if a school doesn't think it worthwhile to remedy the situation among young people, the problem of self-segregation will continue to perpetuate itself for years to come.

MIKE B

In second grade I was diagnosed as having a seizure disorder that has diminished through high school but nevertheless remains a constant threat.

. . . Although having epileptic seizures is dreadful, they have become valuable to me because I have learned a lot and in many ways have become a stronger person. I haven't enjoyed the years in which epilepsy has been part of my life, but I appreciate their value and have grown proud of the way I learned to conduct myself. I stayed strong academically and came to realize just how important my education is. The fact that I was able to excel academically during a period of time which was really very hard has built up my confidence. I came to understand that being educated was one of the values I considered most important, especially being educated about the epileptic seizures that were shaping my life.

Most important was that I made up my mind to cure myself of epilepsy by becoming more informed about it. I really couldn't cure the disease itself, but I could learn to live with it by understanding all there is to know. I have spent countless hours online reading descriptions of other epileptics and their problems. I sent questions to doctors and other experts in the field. With the help of the Epilepsy Research Foundation, I set up a web page and placed appeals on Craig's List, through which I was able to raise funds. Twice in high school, I exceeded my goal of $1,000 per year. By sharing my experiences with other epileptics I made friends and found ways of dealing with it.

. . . In the beginning I wouldn't talk about my problem and even forbade my parents to mention that it existed. I was embarrassed and ashamed. But now I am more open socially and have learned to communicate with and trust my friends. Epilepsy is no longer a stigma; it's a way of life.

MIKE A

In the media and elsewhere, teenagers are portrayed as naturally rebellious, troublemaking, impulsive, irresponsible risk-takers. I think it's time to put an end to this hostile stereotype. Whatever we are, we teenagers reflect our parents. We are no sicker and no healthier than they are. If we seem rude and wild, then look at the adults who have raised us. They drink, smoke, take drugs, steal, lie, act irresponsibly. The difference may be that they have learned to disguise it better, to hide their sins under a veneer of civility.

. . . I'm sick and tired of being pegged as a reckless teenager, sick and tired of being harassed by police when I hang with friends in front of the movie theater on Friday nights, sick and tired of being watched like a criminal when I enter a shop or department store, sick and tired of being treated like dirt by adults who are no better (or worse) than we are.

. . . The sad truth is that we judge adults more generously than they judge us. Overall, we are more open-minded, honest, generous, and accepting of diversity. Taken all together, that is a good omen for society of the future.

The "Significant Person" Question

Indicate a person who has had a significant influence on you, and describe that influence.

Most applicants responding to this prompt write about someone they know—a parent, a teacher, coach, or counselor. Many students also choose a brother or sister, their boss at work, a member of the clergy, or a friend whose influence changed them in some important way.

Not long ago, a Chinese girl who had been in the U.S. only a short time wrote about her fondness for her non-English speaking father, describing how she communicated with him about art, which was non-verbal. "Father" essays are common, but this one impressed admissions officials for its acknowledgment of tenderness mingled with distance. Sometimes the subject of "significant person" essays are long-time acquaintances, at other times someone who has stepped briefly into the applicant's life—a guide on a river trip through the Grand Canyon, for example, or a librarian who recommended an eye-opening book.

You need not choose a person you know or who knows you. A celebrity, a political figure, an athlete, an author, a poet, or a musician whose work you admire—these are just a handful of the people who may have left a significant mark on you. The subject of your essay may be living or dead, male or female, famous, notorious, or anonymous. Essays have been written on the 9/11 hijackers, for instance, and on the firefighters who died in the World Trade Center. A high school senior who loved deer hunting wrote a winning essay about the influence of the unknown person who invented the bow and arrow.

If you choose this question, here are some guidelines to follow.

DO . . .

✓ Consider what your choice of person says about you.

✓ Pick a person whose influence you can fully explain.

✓ Place your emphasis not on the person, but on the nature of that person's influence on you.

✓ Focus on one or two important influences, rather than on several minor ones.

DON'T . . .

✗ Pick a person whose influence is negative—unless you can show that you've resisted or overcome that influence.

✗ Turn the person into a saint; most humans are . . . well, *human*.

✗ Be excessively sappy or sentimental about your influential person.

✗ Forget to show very specific examples of your subject's influence on you.

Excerpts from Answers That Worked

MARNI G

When I was very young my mother introduced me to the world of the printed page, a world as crucial to my existence as breathing. She smothered me with tales of Dr. Seuss and the adventures of Strawberry Shortcake. My dreams were filled with colorful, exciting sagas that my subconscious recreated from bedtime stories.

After a while, I became frustrated with my dependence on my mother for entrance into fantasy land. I wanted to give myself this pleasure, to own these words. My brain strived to make sense of the masses of letters so I could read by myself.

Before long, I conquered this barrier, one that had kept me from experiencing this primary form of pure bliss that was known to me at this point in life. I had achieved the extraordinary—I could read. . . .

. . . I am no longer able to devote every spare moment consuming an endless supply of wonderful books. Yet, literature has become my secret addiction. I steal time from such urgent matters like writing term papers and prepping for exams and rendezvous briefly with authors like Shakespeare, Jane Austen, and Ayn Rand. During moments of an increasingly busy schedule I indulge in just two or three pages of my obsession at a time. Although I've become accustomed to soaking up small doses of heavenly passion, in the back of my mind I still long for the uncomplicated world in which the Cat in the Hat is the ruler and Green Eggs and Ham the official meal.

AILEEN K

Carleton spit at me because I told him he couldn't spit at other kids. Then he fell on the grass, screamed profanities, and threw rocks. The camp director stood by, watching.

I was eight weeks into my ten-week job as counselor at Boynton Valley, a residential camp for children with emotional and behavioral problems, and by that time I had become inured to bed-wetting and spitting and had learned to shrug off derogatory comments about my mother. I had begun to see the endearing personalities that children like Carleton possess.

Carleton is a crack baby with cerebral palsy and ADHD. His hyperactivity is astounding, and his inappropriate behavior is ceaseless. Countless times I watched the smallest incident drive Carleton into a spitting, cursing fit of hysteria. Yet beneath his tantrums is an adorable boy who seeks love and attention. . . .

. . .When camp ended, I was completely unprepared to leave Carleton. I couldn't face sending him back to his myriad of foster mothers and multitudes of schools. Camp showed Carleton consistency, and with it, his behavior improved. Temper tantrums became less frequent, and spitting was reduced to a reaction to anger rather than an attention-getting scheme. Leaving camp, I cried for all my campers, for sadness that they had to go back to families that neglected or abused them, and for the happiness that each of them had enjoyed at camp. . . . Getting on the bus, Carleton whispered to me, "Will you play with me forever?" I smiled regretfully and said, "I wish I could, Carleton. I wish I could."

Carleton's birthday was yesterday. I called but couldn't speak to him because he was away for the weekend with his birth mother. I hung up the phone, saddened, hoping that there are other people in the world who are ready to love Carleton as I do, and to remind him of the success he could achieve.

CHRISTINA S

My father has given me many wonderful gifts. Because of him, I am tall, green-eyed, well-coordinated, and pretty good in school. But he also gave me something that for a long time I could have done without: a full head of bright red hair. "Why couldn't I have been born a brunette, like my sister?" I asked. Instead, I always stood out like a ripe tomato in a fresh green salad.

The reason I especially disliked my hair when I was younger was because I'd be called names like "Red" and "Reddy Foxx" and "OJ" and "Carrot Top." Many times these nicknames would stick and I would lose my identity as Christina and become "The Redhead."

When I finally reached the age when I no longer wanted to be a clone of everyone else, I realized that my hair distinguished me from others.

This was a turning point for me. I started to think that I was unique, and as much as I hate to admit it, I began to relish the attention I got. . . . Now I use my red hair as the basis of my individuality. This discovery has led to a new sense of confidence. It has affected the way I see myself. I began to speak out in class and in groups instead of retiring shyly into the background. I can now speak with assurance in front of groups, enabling me to become involved more fully in school, community, and church activities. . . .

Another good thing that has come from what I considered the traumatic experiences of being teased at an early age is that I am more aware of the feelings of others, and I often find myself defending people from being ridiculed. I now see my red hair as an important part of my personality. And if someone says, "Hey, look at that redhead," I smile and say to myself, "Hey, thanks, Dad."

CHITA A

My mother has been the single most influential person in my life. She brought me to the United States from Puerto Rico soon after she and my father were divorced. She taught me English as a second language, but she also taught me never to forget where I came from. My mother did everything to make sure I stuck to my roots. She enrolled me in a bilingual school and cooked only Puerto Rican dishes. She spoke to me only in Spanish. Not only did I learn to dance salsa, I developed a great sense of pride to be part of Puerto Rican culture.

. . . As I've grown up I cannot thank my mother enough for what she instilled in me. It is very hard to be proud of your background if you are a minority in the United States. If you are a woman it is even harder. Due to the huge amount of discrimination towards non-whites, I used to feel discouraged and wondered how I could possibly contribute to the world. But I looked at my mother and saw what is possible. She is not only an extremely successful attorney, she is a woman, and she is Puerto Rican. Because of her efforts, I am confident that by having faith in my gender, my heritage, and myself, I can accomplish anything.

The "Important Influence" Question

Describe a character in fiction, a historical figure, or a creative work (as in art, music, science, etc.) that has had an influence on you, and explain that influence.

This is much like the previous question, but instead of choosing a real person, you may write about someone who doesn't exist except in a book, play, film, television show, or even in your imagination. The possibilities are endless. Just think of characters you've met in novels, movies, and TV shows. In recent years, "The Sopranos" and "Sex in the City" have inspired an astounding number of essays. In general, though, it may be smart to avoid characters in books widely read in high school, although the last word is yet to be written about Hester Prynne, Huck Finn, and Holden Caulfield. The same applies to historical figures. For every essay written on individuals such as Abigail Adams and Rosa Parks, a dozen are written each year about more prominent figures like Abraham Lincoln and Martin Luther King

Writing about a creative work gives you a chance to show a side of you not evident elsewhere on your application. Art buffs have writen essays about artists who have influenced their work. One student studied the paintings of Winslow Homer and visited sites where Homer traveled and painted. Another discussed the impact on her work of a single painting by the American artist Edward Hopper. Still another identified Ansel Adams as the most significant force in her growth as a photographer. A would-be cartoonist singled out the influence of Charles Schulz, the creator of "Peanuts." Classical composers, the Beatles, Courtney Love, punk rockers Arctic Monkeys, and many other music-makers have also served as essay subjects. Again, however, it's not the choice of person that counts. What matters more is how applicants use their essays to convey what's in their hearts and minds.

DO . . .

✓ Keep in mind that your choice of subject reflects your values, your level of thinking, your creativity, even your sense of humor.

✓ Focus not on the person, but on the person's influence on you.

✓ Analyze the influence and fully explain its importance to you.

✓ Include details about how the subject has made a meaningful difference in your life.

DON'T . . .

✗ Choose a character solely to impress your readers.

✗ Write on a person apt to be chosen by lots of other applicants, such as current movie or TV heroes, or characters in novels and plays studied in school.

✗ Pick a person whose influence has faded or is short-lived.

Excerpts from Answers That Worked

GLENNA A

Through high school I have been taught by approximately 50 different teachers. All of them have had some influence on me, some negative and some positive. The most influential one, however, does not exist in reality. That person is a composite of the best teachers I have had, the one who embodies all the best features in the group.

It doesn't matter to me if that teacher is young or old, single or married, experienced or a beginner. What counts is that s/he knows what s/he is talking about, presents lively and captivating lessons, uses language that is understandable, combines lecture with class discussions, gives homework that is not a waste of time, returns tests and papers promptly, never puts students down, likes to have fun, is willing to really listen to and respect kids' opinions, doesn't play favorites, grades fairly, occasionally reveals his/her personal life, and appreciates the difficulties and understands the problems of growing up in the 21st century.

Why am I telling you this? Because my experience with 50 teachers has taught me that if I like the teacher and the teacher seems to like me, I'd go to the ends of the earth to learn, to please him or her, to get the most I possibly can out of the course. . . .

. . . Oh, yes, one final qualification: if the teacher is male, I'd like him to be cute.

MORGAN J

The timing was perfect. I had just switched from violin to viola, an instrument I was excited about, and so my mind was open to change. For whatever reason on that spring morning, my English teacher played a recording of the "Ode to Joy" from Beethoven's Ninth Symphony for the class. I knew the piece, of course, and could pluck out the theme on the piano, but on this day in English class I basically listened to the piece for the first time in my life.

. . . The music didn't float over my ears as classical music usually did. It came right at me. It barged into my life like a tsunami. Its spell stayed with me and gave me an outlook on classical music that has never left me. That morning in English class I was turned into a musician.

. . . Since that encounter with the "Ninth" I've become obsessed with having others share the experience of having classical music possess them. I have started preparing a program with a friend which we call "Classical is Cool," meant to teach elementary school kids about this music.

. . . I am convinced that discussing such pieces as the "Ninth," Dvorak's "American" String Quartet, and Tchaikovsky's Violin Concerto with kids, talking about how the music makes them feel, what images, or even just colors, it evokes, will show them than classical music is much more than background noise. Rather, like nothing else, the music of Bach and Brahms can be a transforming experience.

DORE D

. . . As I approached the narrow door that led into the world of Anne Frank's secret annex, I grew solemn. From the moment I entered the house, I was transformed. No longer an American tourist in Amsterdam, I became a thirteen-year-old Jewish girl being forced into hiding to escape the horrors of Nazi occupation. Yet, I could hardly begin to imagine staying month after month in a tiny apartment, remaining silent most of the time, being ever fearful of discovery.

. . . Anne's room moved me the most. It was cold, dark, gloomy, not the least bit feminine. Anne's pictures still clung to the rust-yellow walls. "How different from my room," I whispered to my mother, thinking of the warm glow of art nouveau lights that lit up my framed posters of Monet, Matisse, Mucha, and Manet.

. . . As I stood once more in the sunshine outside Anne Frank's house, I reflected on my visit. I did not understand the kind of hatred of a race or religion that would cause humans to treat each other so brutally. As Anne did, I enjoy watching the progressions of the seasons, having intimate talks with friends, and envisioning what the future might hold. She, along with countless other Jews, was deprived of these simples pleasures, however.

. . . As a young woman approaching college, I knew that I could not solve the world's problems. But I couldn't help thinking that my brief look at Anne's world would make me more sensitive to others and more aware of their needs. Out in the open air, the words of John Wesley's poem flowed through my mind:

"Do all the good you can,/ In all the ways you can,/ In all the places you can,/ At all the times you can,/ To all the people you can,/ As long as ever you can."

CLAIRE W

(The lights dim, the theme music begins, the audience settles down.)

"I am Betty Parris. I am Betty Parris, I am . . ." Lock the audience out. Don't look at them. Concentrate inside. I am Betty Parris. What are my intentions? I want power. I want to be stronger than Abigail. Why? She can manipulate me, and she can twist my emotions to fit the intricate mindgames she plays. I'm cold as ice, and I feel my nerves hardening. Slowly all my good intentions will seep away into my surroundings and I will be purely evil. There's no going back now. Murder is final. I'll sacrifice whatever or whoever I need to, but I will prevail. Now I am Betty Parris . . . .

Taking a role on stage is turning yourself into someone else. After performing in *The Crucible*, I realized that becoming a character means incorporating that person into who I am. As I played Betty Parris, her traits became mine, and her deep dark secrets were those I created. In a sense, I became an extension of myself.

Developing the character of Betty led me to encounter something disturbing. I had to dig into myself, dredge up my worst points, and magnify them in order to make my performance effective. The result frightened me. While on stage I felt tense. My teeth were clenched, my hands balled into fists, my shoulders almost shook from strain. Bodily movements became more forceful, as though each action was full of the desire to lash out. My anger towards the character of Abigail was so profound that her touch made me cringe. I truly wished she would die.

Having turned into Betty, I felt a capacity for cold hatred, a sensation I had never before experienced. How could the potential for raw violence exist in me? Probably because it exists to some degree in everyone, but few of us notice its presence unless it has to be dug up. Even scarier was the idea that I had rooted out a wickedness inside me not by accident but on purpose, as though I always knew it was there. I am glad to have found it. I'm not an evil person, but for the first time I could feel the place that true hatred springs from, and I became sensitive to a potentially dangerous emotion within myself. Emerging from the role of Betty Parris, I recognize and continue to work at removing this terrible cancer inside me.

The "Diversity" Question

A range of academic interests, personal perspectives, and life experiences adds much to the educational mix. Given your personal background, describe an experience that illustrates what you would bring to the diversity in a college community, or an encounter that demonstrated the importance of diversity to you.

Admissions officials like to bring to their campuses a diverse mix of bright, confident, and upbeat people who will help make the college a stimulating place for the next four years. This question offers you a chance to explain how you can contribute to that diversity.

If you are an accomplished debater, high-diver, computer nerd, dancer, bird-watcher—or if you have any other special skill or passion, you have a ready-made essay topic. Just tell the college what you can do. Because the needs of every college change from time to time, any special ability or interest can become your ticket to admission. If, for instance, most of the drummers in the college's marching band are seniors, you can bet that admissions people will be asked to keep a sharp lookout for academically qualified high school drummers.

You might also add to a college's diversity on the basis of where you happen to live and how you spent your childhood. Colleges hope to draw students from all over the map. Typically, an East Coast college will look kindly on an academically able applicant who grew up roping calves on a ranch in Idaho or one who lived for years in a self-sufficient community in the Cascade Mountains of Oregon.

Applicants from high schools in the suburbs of Boston, New York, or other metropolitan areas can't depend on geographical diversity to help their applications. They need to highlight their uniqueness in other ways. Margerita A, born in Colombia and raised in a blue-collar home in Roxbury, Massachusetts, wrote that she would be the first in her family to attend college. Paul T from White Plains, New York, is an Eagle Scout and an auxiliary volunteer at the local airport where, after learning about flying and air safety, he'll start flight training for a pilot's license. Jake G, from suburban New Jersey, has bred, sold, and shown pedigreed Maine coon cats since he was 12 years old. In other words, life experiences and interests provide good material for answering the "diversity" question.

DO . . .

✓ Choose a topic that highlights your individuality.

✓ Show how your interest or talent has enriched your life.

✓ Show specifically how you can contribute to the diversity of the college.

✓ Write about an academic interest only if you've done more than take a high school course in the subject.

DON'T . . .

✗ Pick this topic unless you've thought carefully and honestly about the importance of diversity to you.

✗ Go overboard; be mindful that a thin line separates uniqueness from eccentricity.

✗ Choose a rare, off-the-wall experience to illustrate your commitment to diversity.

✗ Present yourself as a fanatic nonconformist or a rebel to prove your diversity.

Excerpts from Answers That Worked

KATE G

As "Aqua-Girl" (half human, half fish), I would undoubtedly add diversity to a college located in the middle of corn and soybean fields over a thousand miles from an ocean. Last summer I became a certified PADI Junior Open Water Diver. So far, I have completed seven dives off the California coast and fifteen dives at the Galapagos Islands during Christmas. I swam with the turtles, rays, and even a whale shark! Three years ago, when my family and I went to the Great Barrier Reef, I was too young to scuba dive, as I was under thirteen, but snorkeling on the surface, I could see the scuba divers with the giant grouper and other sea creatures. . . .

From an early age, the human side of me has loved fishing. I used to tag along with my father to the local man-made fishing pond and try to "roll-cast" with his fly-rods. The first fishing trip our family took was to Alaska. There we caught almost everything you can find in the seafood section of a supermarket. From then on, fishing rods were part of almost every family vacation. The biggest fish I ever caught was a 140-pound tarpon in Florida. Some of my other fishing adventures have included salmon fishing where the Columbia River meets the Pacific, casting for blues on Cape Cod, lobstering in the Gulf of Mexico, and trawling for fish in Australia and Malaysia.

. . . As someone who has spent most of her life near, on, or in the sea, it may strike you as odd that I'd like to go to college so far inland. But that is just the point. In college I want to be exposed to the unfamiliar, the out of the ordinary, the *diverse*.

   . . . and by the way, I've read <u>Moby Dick</u>— twice!

KARYN R

I once thought I could change the world, and the paper tacked to my church bulletin board offered me the perfect opportunity. "Volunteers Wanted," it said. The fine print said that poor people in the town of D_____, New York had been given notice of eviction from their houses, which had been condemned by the government as "unfit for human habitation." Volunteers were needed to go upstate and help fix up the existing housing to prevent the displacement of dozens of families.

. . . The poverty of the people and the enormity of the job hit me like a slap across the face when we arrived in D_____. Besides being hot, unbearably hot, the town was disgustingly dirty and run-down. A scrawny dog barked at me. Barefoot children stood in the dust and stared at me with sad, vacant eyes as I wondered what on earth I was doing there while all my friends were hedonistically shagging rays at the beach back home and having fun.

. . . Hopelessness surrounded me, yet my minister's hope could never be dashed. He smiled and urged us on. "Let's do it," he said. "Let's save these houses from the dozer." His spirit made me feel ashamed of my pessimism, so I pitched in with all my might to clean up the squalid, rat- and cockroach-infested shacks. . . .

. . . I no longer believe that I can change the world. But I won't give up trying. I saw the progress made with my own hands during six weeks of intensive labor. I have left a tiny corner of the world in better shape than when I found it. I will continue my campaign to help my fellow man. I hope to join the Peace Corps after college. Wherever they send me, I'll go with a much greater understanding of mankind and of myself.

NEWT F

"Do you have any siblings?" someone asked.

"Yes, I have one," I replied, "a brother."

"How old?"

"Twenty."

"What college does he go to?"

"Um, he's not in college. He's retarded, um, and he goes to high school with me."

"Oh, I see."

I've had conversations like this hundreds of times. Yet each one brews new emotions. Sometimes I'm proud to have a retarded brother.

At other times, I'm embarrassed and feel I've been given a raw deal. "Why me?" I ask myself. Why is Kevin older than me, yet I am his big brother? Why isn't he taking me to a party at his college instead of me walking him to the bus every morning because he's scared of the neighbor's dog. . . .

. . . Then I turn it around and realize what a huge part of my life Kevin is, and how he has changed me as a person. He has made me more caring than the average male teen, and I am more open and aware of others' emotions.

. . . I can do so many things that he can't. This is hard because he is envious of me. Whether I'm running out to a club meeting, playing soccer, rushing to band practice or play rehearsal at school, or just going out with friends, I will pause, and during that pause a guilty feeling comes over me. I can't blame him for it, but it's tinged slightly with regret—or is it resentment? Before his twentieth birthday party, he asked if some of my friends would come. I knew they wouldn't, but I could not disappoint him. "Maybe next year," I said.

. . . I try to soothe his envy of me by suggesting we do things together and choosing something that he can do. Bowling, for one. We go often to the local alley where he is known as "Big Kev." The other day after a game he said sadly, "I didn't do too good today." I put my arm over his shoulder and in a half whisper replied with words I try to live by: "You did your best. You'll get 'em next time, Kev, you'll get 'em next time." Deep inside I know this may not be true. But there will be hundreds of games in the future, hundreds of afternoons spent together, hundreds of times when his ball might, just might roll down the middle of the alley and knock down every pin. I look forward to each and every one of them.

DREW G

Last summer I ran headlong into diversity and it changed my life. Until then, I didn't think much about what would become of me. I simply assumed that I'd go to college, get a job, get married, have kids, and live happily ever after in a pleasant suburban town such as my own. How this fantasy would come to pass I hadn't a clue. I didn't think about it. Like everything else in my life, I just assumed it would happen naturally if I continued going to school, did my homework, said "no" to drugs, and went to church. Somehow I took it for granted that a good life would be provided.

Seventeen years of being shielded from reality were shattered on my first morning as a caddy at the local country club. While waiting for my assignment, I began to eavesdrop on the conversations in the caddy yard. One of my fellow caddies told of how he got drunk last night and began a bar brawl. Another told of trying to cash a welfare check that he had found in the street. Still another described how he struggled to keep his family going on food stamps and tips from caddying. I was shocked, not because of their style of living, but that these grown men had no dreams, no goal in life to work towards. They seemed content to collect handouts from the government and to work at a dead-end job carrying the golf bags for club members. . . . They lived day by day and never thought of tomorrow.

. . . Suddenly I saw myself twenty years from now sitting in the caddy yard exchanging anecdotes with others just like them. I was shocked. I could not live their lifestyle. The monotony of it would kill me before the alcohol would. I began to see school as more than just homework and tests without purpose, but as a way to improve myself. I found within me a drive and determination I had not known existed. I resolved to do better. I realized that going to college was more than something to do for four years. It was a necessity, an invaluable tool that would help me to magnify my determination to make something of myself and use my new-found ambition.

The "Open" Question
A topic of your choice

If the first five questions leave you cold, here's your chance to invent a fresh, original question and to write a response that tells colleges whatever you want to say about yourself—no holds barred.

By choosing your own topic, you are free to send in an essay you've already written for a non-Commonapp college. You wouldn't be the first to do so. College admissions officials know the pressures you face during application season. They won't think less of you and may even be impressed by your efficiency.

Another tactic is simply to adapt one or more of the previous prompts, turning it into a topic you're burning to write about.

DO . . .

- ✓ Remember the purpose of an application essay—to tell a college about your experiences, goals, personality, and priorities.

- ✓ Write an essay that only you can write because of who you are and what you've experienced.

- ✓ Pick a single topic and stick to it. By discussing a variety of topics, you'll dilute your essay's impact.

- ✓ Use a fresh, honest, independent voice that puts the reader inside your head.

DON'T . . .

- ✗ Refer to other parts of the application. Let your essay stand alone as a separate piece of work.

- ✗ Whine or whimper (about grades, a bad roommate at a summer program, the other kids on the prom committee who didn't pull their weight, etc.) "Poor me" essays are doomed.

- ✗ Write an essay for the sole purpose of attracting attention. It will most likely appear out of context and confuse readers about who you really are.

✗ Write more than is asked for; don't go over the space allotted or suggested by the college. When in doubt, keep it short.

Excerpts from Answers That Worked

CHRISTIE G

Question: Would you like time to run backwards in order to undo yesterday's mistakes?

Answer: Before signing up for the possibility of running time backwards, I would insist on knowing the ground rules. I would gladly embrace reversing time if the policy contained certain provisions, but I would turn down the opportunity to participate if other rules applied.

First, I would need to know whether my memory of the future would stay with me in the past. Would I go back knowing everything I know now, or would I be starting from scratch? If going back to sixth grade meant going back to zero and starting over, I say "Forget it!" I would be a masochist to want to relive the nightmares of early adolescence. The agonies of middle school, puberty, disagreements between friends, competition to be cool, and the first tentative experiments with sex, booze, and smoking are not something that I'd like to live through again. Back then I experienced enough anxiety, hair-pulling, and groping from pimple-faced boys to last a lifetime.

However, if I was allowed to go back fully aware of what was to come, and I knew all I know now, it would be hard to resist. From the beginning, I would be much smarter than everyone else, and I would know who would be successful and who would be losers in high school. I would also be fortunate to be able to predict not only important world events like 9/11, but I'd be able to prevent Sarah, my best friend, from getting into a car one weekend in eighth grade and almost being killed in a crash. Soon everyone would be looking up to me as an amazing child prodigy and prophet. People would fuss over me and pay big money for the right to ask for information on everything from the outcome of the Super Bowl (not that I would remember any sports trivia) to tips on the stock market (my father would like that).

. . . There are many other positive aspects to reliving a time I've already gone through. But, as I think more about the consequences, it wouldn't be as wonderful as it seems. Knowing ahead of time what will happen drains the adventure out of living. Anticipating the unknown can be a satisfying emotional high, like the days leading up to an event like the junior prom or receiving my acceptance at my number-one college choice. Discovering new things and dreaming about possibilities is exciting. When I think about conceited people who believe they already know everything (even though they don't), they are bitter, cynical, and bored with life and themselves. I know that I'd feel wretched without the unexpected to look forward to. So, I say leave time as it is. Let the future come with whatever it brings. I am content waiting for it.

SHARON C

> *"Georgiana," said he, "has it never occurred to you that the mark upon your cheek might be removed?"*
>
> *"No, indeed," said she, smiling: but, perceiving the seriousness of his manner, she blushed deeply. "To tell the truth, it has been so often called a charm that I was simple enough to imagine it might be so."*

—Nathaniel Hawthorne, "The Birthmark"

"Are you going to have that big freckle removed from your knee, or what? Don't you hate it?"

The big freckle is actually a tan, oval birthmark located on my right knee, and no, I don't hate it. I like it and won't have it taken off.

But this was not always so. I didn't used to think that having a birthmark was a blessing. I considered it an abhorrence placed on me at birth to make me a freak. I would try to scrape it off or cover it with a bandage. I would beg my father to let me have it removed, but he always said no. It was only as I grew older that my obsession to eliminate my birthmark ceased as I found more important things to concentrate on. I began to regard my birthmark in a new way and think that perhaps it really might be a blessing.

My birthmark helps me with my sense of humor and enables me to laugh at myself. Whenever a person sees the brown mark on my knee, he will stare at it, asking incredulously, "What is that?" I pretend not to know what he's talking about and exclaim, "I was drinking coffee and it must have spilled on me. I hope the stain will wash out." As inane as that sounds, a few people have actually believed me.

I have also made people laugh with the help of my birthmark. I have been a lifeguard for the past two summers and I've challenged myself to get a tan as dark as my birthmark. I never have made it, but I've had fun trying and seeing the looks on people's faces when they see the glob of white zinc I put on my knee to prevent the birthmark from getting darker.

My birthmark gives me courage. I want to prove that this odd mark on my leg won't hinder me in any way. I like to try new things. I'm involved in school, the Student Government, Key Club, Red Cross, sports, and more. I've been to numerous conventions and gone on an exchange to France. Yet, while giving me self-confidence, my birthmark also keeps me humble. After all, it's embarrassing when someone thinks I have dirt on my knee all the time.

My birthmark is also a great conversation piece. I've met new people and had interesting conversations because of it. It has also taught me much about myself and who I am. I'm glad that I have this unique mark. In a way, it is my amulet, a badge of honor that I wear proudly. It makes me different from everyone else. After all, there are few people in this world wearing permanent coffee stains on their leg.

MICHAEL M

"How in the world do you know where anything is in this room, with all this junk?" said my mother one night while I was doing math homework. Putting my books aside, I began to think: "Yeah, I should start getting rid of things I've outgrown."

The next day I started the winnowing process, trying to locate things I didn't want or need any more. I found everything I ever saved from childhood— G.I. Joe action figures in a box, big cartons of Legos, used when I dreamed of becoming an architect; then, I happened upon transformers for toy robots, my Cub Scout manual . . . Finally, I came to a small cigar box labeled PRIVATE. I knew immediately what was inside, but I had to make sure everything was safe. Stuffed into the box were an old silver coin that commemorated Lincoln's birthday, a two dollar bill, and a small Bible. The Bible was falling apart. Inside its cover, under my grandmother's name, was printed in large block letters the name JAMES, my father. It had been my father's Bible when he was a boy. After my grandmother died, it was given to me. Inside in a clear baggie tucked into Deuteronomy was a pressed flower from Granny's funeral. This was the most cherished thing I owned. It wasn't a gift bought at the local toy store; it was a precious part of my life as well as part of my grandmother's and father's lives. They are things that I would never get rid of—never!

. . . And when my mother asks me again, which she inevitably will, to get rid of my junk, I will plainly tell her, "This isn't junk, this is my life."

SEAN N

When my third grade teacher asked me what a philosopher is, all I could answer was "an ancient Greek?" recalling the only instances when I had heard the word. After she explained it, however, I realized that I had indeed known what a philospher is: It is . . . it is . . . ME. It was a shock to learn that as I trekked to and from school each day I myself was a philosopher, someone who takes time just to think. Evidently the practice of philosophy was hardly new, although I had a secret feeling that my search for an "it"—a universal discovery that would revolutionize the world and bring everyone to agreement on all things—had been my invention.

During my walks I often fought off the notion that "it" just didn't exist. There can't be an infinite number of ways to see life, I sometimes thought, but now I believe that that *is* the secret. There are infinite ways to view reality. Everything is but a perception. I recall one day sitting in ninth grade English class, the warm sun bathing my back, and hearing only a mumble of voices which became people throwing the words "fact" and "opinion" at each other. These people, disputing what was fact and what opinion, helped me conclude that there is just no difference. No facts, no opinions, just perceptions. I felt so enlightened; this could be that universal truth I was seeking. I gave the idea a name: "Perceptionism."

. . . Perceptionism has many implications when dealing with people. Nobody is ever wrong or right, or stupid or intelligent; they simply have a different point of view, a different perception. For example, when I work with children after school in the Day Care Center, I must be flexible and try to think as they do. When dealing with my grandmother, who has Alzheimer's, I must free my imagination to picture where her mind is at a given moment. Since I am an actor, this is especially important. An actor must be able to understand people enough to feel as they do. Therefore, there is much to learn from and about people by following the theory of perceptionism.

. . . Almost every day my theory lets me discover more about people, for there is nothing more interesting than the human mind. Fortunately for me, the world is filled with people for me to find, and I've been given a life to find them in. And if I ever get tired of "finding," I may end up settling down on a little farm, in some postcard-forsaken place to take the time just to think.

Supplements to the Common Application

Many Commonapp colleges want you to answer additional questions on a supplementary form. These supplements often include essay questions, some of them labeled "optional." Don't believe it. Show the college that you're dead set on being admitted. Answer every supplemental question, optional or not, as fully and enthusiastically as you can.

Although supplementary questions may differ in detail from one college to another, they fall loosely into the following categories: (1) Why go to college, and why here? (2) Who are you? (3) What is important to you? and (4) Is there anything else you would like to say about yourself?

In the sample questions and topics listed in this chapter, you may not find the exact question your college asks, but you'll probably recognize one that comes close.

Why Go to College? Why Here?

From questions about your plans for the future, colleges hope to discern your route for the next four years. What will the college experience mean to you? Will you study, or will you party? Have you thought about why you're going to college at all? Expecting a look at your educational map, colleges often make inquiries such as these:

—Why do you want to go to college?
—Why do you want to go to this college, in particular?
—What are your career objectives, and how will college help you achieve them?
—How will this college help you fulfill your goals and aspirations?
—What will your presence add to this college?

No one answer to such questions is preferable to another. If you aim to be a dentist or a Washington lawyer, that's fine. Yet no college seeks to fill its classrooms with only one type of student. In the main, colleges try to keep their enrollments balanced. It's not a weakness, therefore, to admit that you don't know how you want to spend the rest of your life. College is for exploring. In fact, liberal arts students frequently come to campuses with receptive and open minds. More than likely, they'll rummage through many of the offerings on which a college has built its reputation.

As you explain your intentions to a college, consider these essay-writing hints:

DO . . .

✓ Answer the question being asked, not the one you'd like to answer.

✓ Before writing a word, scrutinize the college's offerings. If you expect to major in, say, ecology, be sure the college has an environmental studies program.

✓ Think hard about what *you* hope to get out of college, avoiding clichés, such as "I want an education," "I want to get a good, well-paying job," and "I want to be a success in my chosen field."

✓ Try to figure out why this college appeals to you. Did the college representatives make it sound exciting? Did you visit the campus and fall in love with the place? Is there a particular program that attracts your interest?

✓ Focus on educational or personal reasons for going to college, not on social, economic, or family reasons.

DON'T . . .

✗ Use flattery. All colleges already know how good they are.

✗ Stress that you love the college's location, size, or appearance. By applying there, you have implied that those characteristics are acceptable to you.

✗ Tell a college that it's your "safe" school.

✗ Write that you're going to college because your family expects you to.

Finally, don't take any of these precautions as the last word in application essay writing. Use them at your discretion. Don't ignore them, though, unless you have a sound reason for doing so. Jim D, for example, came right out and told Bowdoin he wanted to go there precisely because of its location. "Like Thoreau," Jim wrote, "I feel most alive near wild streams and forests."

Dow T's visit to Yale convinced him to apply. In his essay, he reinforces his commitment by referring to specific people and groups he met during a weekend visit to the campus: "From the Whiffenpoofs, who performed at my high school last year, to the activist crowd I met in Dwight Hall during my visit last April, I sense that Yale is packed with people who've 'got passion' and are 'smart with heart.' My friend, David Kim, a senior at Yale, wishes he could stay another year; his college has become his family. Mr. Luckett from the admissions office told me, 'Yale doesn't accept the smartest—only the best.' And no kidding—I want to be a member of the Purple Crayon Club."

Answers That Worked

Marian T's afterschool work in a fabric shop inspired her love of fashion and developed her flair for design. "In college," Marian wrote, "I plan to major in fine arts."

David B studied four languages in high school. Because of his bent toward languages and foreign cultures, he wants a career in international affairs as a businessman or diplomat, but he said, "A stint in the Peace Corps will come first."

Lisa C loves to read. "I can't imagine a career more suited to me than librarian in a school or a public library," she wrote.

Wendy W has wide and wandering interests. Last year it was dance, this year it is community service. Wendy thinks of college as a place for "accumulating more interests, for meeting people, for working hard, and, ultimately, for finding a niche in life to fill."

Andy S has always taken the hardest courses. He doesn't know why, except that doing well in tough courses has made him feel good. "I hope to continue feeling good in college," he quipped.

Deena R admires one of her high school English teachers. Since he's told her wonderful stories of Williams College, she'd like to go there, too. "I plan to major in English," she wrote, "and find out if Mr. Stern's stories are true."

Karen S's "most joyful and gratifying high school experience" has been working with mentally retarded children. In college she'll major in special education.

Mark D lost his father and a brother last year. Yet he has retained his essential optimism. He wrote that "there is still a promise in life for me. There are so many things that I have not yet experienced, but inevitably must. That's why I want to go to college."

Don Z has met many people through playing guitar at festivals and nightspots. He thrives on people whose style of living differs from his. Don asked, "What better place than a giant university is there for finding a variety of people?"

Becky B is thinking of a career in acting. She expects a college education to help her become a more complete person. "My wish," she wrote, "is not only to be a good actor but also a good person, and my belief is that they might be the same thing."

Who Are You?

Colleges have heard what others think of you—teachers, counselors, interviewers. With self-assessment questions, they hope to learn what you think of yourself. Do you know who you are? Are you aware of how others react to you? Would you like to change in some way? Self-knowledge is often thought to be a prerequisite for understanding the world, and an essay that demonstrates that you know yourself will give your application a big boost. To check the depth of your insight, colleges ask questions like these:

—What is important to you?
—How would you describe yourself as a human being?
—How might a freshman roommate describe you?
—Write your own recommendation to college.
—If you could strengthen one aspect of yourself, what would it be? Why?
—What quality do you like best in yourself? What quality do you like least?
—Imagine yourself as a book or other object. How would people react to you?
—What makes you different from other people?

In your response, readers hope to find clues to your personality. Unless you present yourself as a bizarre monster, they won't necessarily care whether you are soft-spoken or loud, a realist or a dreamer, a liberal or a rock-hard conservative. They'll give you short shrift, however, if they think you are a fake. Above all, then, in writing "who are you?" essays, be truthful with yourself—as truthful as you've ever been before.

> Telling the truth doesn't mean you must bare your soul.

Telling the truth doesn't mean you must bare your soul and disclose your deepest secrets. Colleges don't need to know about your sex life, psychiatric treatment, or drug and drinking problems. On the other hand, you needn't portray yourself as a saint. Students have written successful essays about their cynicism, frustration, greed, and favorite vices. "Every year," says Barbara Jan Wilson, formerly the dean of admission at Wesleyan and now a university vice president, "we get an essay or two about a student's first sexual experience, written as a literal response to the 'significant experience' question." Wilson says, "Don't do this. It shows poor judgment and is not relevant to admission to college." In the end, let good taste govern your choice of material. If you have doubts, switch topics. Jenny G wrote an essay about a family drug problem, thought the better of it afterward, and wrote another, highlighting her good judgment.

DO . . .

- ✓ Answer the question that is asked.
- ✓ Be as honest as you can. Search for qualities you really have, not those you wish for.
- ✓ Emphasize specific, observable qualities that show your distinctive personality. Imagine that your reader will someday have to pick you out in a crowd.
- ✓ Illustrate your qualities with specific examples. Use telling anecdotes to support your opinions of yourself.
- ✓ Ask people who know you well whether they agree with your self-analysis.

DON'T . . .

- ✗ Be evasive. Stand up for what you think about yourself.
- ✗ Be too cute or coy. Sincerity is preferable.
- ✗ Choose a characteristic merely to impress the college.
- ✗ Write everything you know about yourself. Focus on one or two of your outstanding qualities.
- ✗ Write an essay fit for *The Daily E! Message Board Threads.*

Remember that you can violate every rule and still write a compelling essay. Just be aware of the perils.

Answers That Worked

Suzannah R thinks of herself as a dynamo in danger of burning out by age twenty. She can't control her energy level. She's impatient and often intolerant of others' laid-back attitudes. She added, "As I have grown older, I feel I am learning to accept other people's shortcomings."

David V said, "The most important fact to know about me is that I am a Black person in a White society." David considers himself an outsider and expects to continue feeling alienated as long as racial prejudice exists.

Ellen E contrasted her goofing off early in high school ("personal problems and just plain stupidity") with her productive junior and senior years. In effect, she was reborn during the summer between tenth and eleventh grades.

Allison R has fought shyness all her life. She recounted three moments in her life when shyness defeated her. In contrast, she told of three recent incidents that have helped to raise her self-esteem.

Steve M sees himself as a latter-day Clarence Darrow, always standing in defense of the little guy, often taking the minority point of view in class just to generate a little controversy. If others consider him obnoxious, he claimed, "it's a small price to pay for a life full of heated debates and discussions."

Adam L works 25 to 30 hours a week during the school year loading and unloading trucks for the family business. He says that working such long hours "means I don't get to 'live' as much." But he takes solace in thinking that he knows the value of hard work and when he graduates from college, he'll be better prepared for the real world.

John K sees himself as a character in a movie. When he's alone he pretends he's Leonardo DiCaprio, playing the role of a Millennial generation bachelor. He even hums background film music when he's driving and jogging.

Brendan B is a gourmet cook. He loves to eat. "You are what you eat," he believes, so he defined himself by the food he enjoys most. From meat and potatoes, for example, he has gained a strong will. From French sauces, he has derived a subtle sense of humor.

Nicole W is a perfectionist. From schoolwork to keeping her room in order, she cannot allow herself to do anything shabbily or incomplete. She is worried about "getting a slob for a college roommate."

Dena P, a gymnast since age eight, wrote that she "works like a demon" to be number one. Ever striving for perfection, she added, "I know now that when it comes to making commitments, I can be ready to make them."

Doug M is an adopted Korean orphan. He sees himself as a child of two cultures. Although a double identity causes confusion in others, he feels "more fortunate and richer" than his American classmates.

Jennifer B loves computers. Everything about computers comes so easily and naturally to her that she said, "I sometimes think that I must have been born in a Dell Computer factory. Instead of brains, maybe I have memory boards and microcircuitry inside my head."

Would You Tell Us a Story About Yourself?

Telling stories is a most ordinary thing to do. After school you tell what happened that day. You tell friends what Donna said to Fred and how Kathy felt afterward.

The story you write for a college application isn't expected to be like a superbly crafted tale by Poe or O'Henry, just an autobiographical account of an experience. It should tell about something that happened and what it meant to you. A good story both entertains and informs the reader. A story written on a college application does even more. It suggests your values, clarifies your attitudes, and, better yet, brings you to life in the admissions office.

Although storytelling possibilities are limitless, application questions usually direct you to identify and discuss a noteworthy time in your life:

> —Write an original essay about a humorous personal experience.
> —What is it that you have done that best reflects your personality?
> —Describe a challenging situation and how you responded.
> —Comment on an experience that helped you discern or define a value you hold.
> —What is the most difficult thing you've ever done?
> —Write about a group endeavor in which you participated, and describe your contribution.

In response to any of these topics, you can write a story about last night or pick an event from the time you were a small child. The experience can have been instantaneous or long-lived, a once-in-a-lifetime occasion or a daily occurrence. It can have taken place in a schoolroom, a ballroom, a mountaintop—anywhere, in fact, including inside your head.

An event need not have been earthshaking to inspire a story. Almost everything you do from the moment you wake up holds possibilities. If you haven't noticed how life is crammed with moments of drama, cast off those blurry lenses and start to look for the hidden realities behind the daily face of things: In a disagreement with your brother, in an encounter with a former girlfriend or boyfriend, or in a teacher's criticism you may find the ingredients for an insightful, dramatic essay. Simply by making a list of ten things that happened yesterday and another ten things that occurred last week, you may trigger more than one essay idea.

> Almost anything you do from the moment you wake up has possibilities.

DO . . .

✓ Answer the question that is asked.

✓ Choose an experience you remember well. Details will make or break your story.

✓ Pick an experience you can dramatize. Let the reader hear people speaking and see people acting!

✓ Focus on a specific incident or event.

✓ Make yourself the central character in the story.

DON'T . . .

✗ Think that a commonplace event can't be turned into an uncommonly good story.

✗ Choose a complicated event unless you can explain it briefly. Fill in background, but focus on what happened.

✗ Bore your readers with a rambling tale that goes nowhere.

✗ Explain your point with a lecture on what the reader is supposed to notice. Let the story make its own point.

Answers That Worked

Ted B collects things: Matchbox cars, license plates, matchbook covers, and rocks. From his hobby he has learned about design, geography, advertising, and geology—and interior decorating, too, for after five years of collecting, he literally wallpapered the foyer of his house with matchbook covers.

Pete S was riding in a car with his brother. At a stoplight a pretty girl in a neighboring car smiled at him. Pete looked away. Afterward, he berated himself and resolved to become more outgoing and more assertive—with mixed results.

Colin V is Catholic. Last year on May 6th his Jewish godson was born. As a result, Colin's eyes have been opened to the world of Jewish customs. "I look at my religion differently now," Colin wrote.

Jenny B's hard-of-hearing grandfather lives with the family. Whenever Jenny tries to help the old man, he rebuffs her. A blowup occurred after Jenny knocked too loudly on his door to summon him to the phone. The incident has caused her to reflect at length on the needs of her grandfather and other aging people.

Mary G, from a middle-class family, works in a slum area soup kitchen with her church group. She'll never be a social reformer, but the work, she claims, has made her "more sensitive to the lives of the poor and homeless."

Roy O's summer at a lake with his father building a cabin gave him time to think about how lucky he was to have been born in the United States into a fairly well-to-do family. "I'll never take the blessings of life for granted again," he wrote.

Liz H and her twin sister Mary have rarely been apart. Lately, Liz has found it necessary to seek her own identity and has taken up running as a way to get away. Her hours of solitude on the road have helped to strengthen the bonds with her sister.

Sandy M says, "Sunday is always spent gathering the scattered fragments of my life." It's the day she uses to catch up on schoolwork, gain some perspective on her social life, make peace with her parents, and look in the mirror for a long time trying to figure out who she is.

Lauren S has always been plagued by insecurity. An offhand remark by an art teacher ("Hey, you're good!") has helped her to build confidence and work that much harder in her courses. She's beginning to see signs of how good she really is.

Lisa R's parents were divorced. The complex legal negotiations that accompanied the split, while painful to her, so fascinated Lisa that she plans to become a lawyer.

Robert S thinks that he has been ostracized at his school because of his ragged appearance. Instead of wearing a jacket and tie to an honor society interview, he showed up in a black leather jacket and torn jeans. The incident heightened his awareness that people are judged by superficialities, not by their character.

What Is Important to You?

Would you rather listen to a Bach cantata or a Metallica album? Would you prefer to blog or spend an afternoon in an art museum? Do you like fast foods or nouvelle cuisine? To a great extent, your preferences define you. Hoping for a glimpse of your taste and your biases, many colleges ask you to write a "choice" essay. Rather than give you a menu of choices, however, they tell you to come up with one of your own—your favorite quotation or word, an historical event you would like to have changed, a significant book you've read:

—What is your favorite quotation? Explain your choice.
—What have you read that has had special significance for you? Explain.
—What is your favorite noun? What does it mean to you?
—If you could invent anything, what would you create? Discuss.
—If you could affect the outcome of human history by changing a particular event, what event would you choose? How would you change it, and why?
—If you could spend an evening with any prominent person—living, deceased, or fictional—whom would you choose, and why?

What you choose when responding to such questions is important. But the rationale for your choice is even more important and should make up the heart of your essay.

The key to writing a forceful response is that your choice has some direct, personal bearing on your life. A quotation from

Shakespeare may sound impressive, but if you pick it only for effect, you'd be better off with a lyric from Shania Twain or a maxim of your grandmother's. If you write on a book, don't limit yourself to school reading. What you've read on your own tells far more about you than any class assignment.

If your first response to a question is, "Oh, that's an easy one!" ask yourself if the same "easy" answer might not be popping into a thousand other minds across the country. Then set your sights on a less obvious answer. Conversations with Columbus, George Washington, and John Lennon have already been written. So have numerous essays about inventing cures for cancer and AIDS. Many students have already written about altering human history by eliminating war, preventing the birth of Hitler, and canceling JFK's trip to Dallas. Frankly, admissions staffers sigh wearily over essays on overused topics.

The good news, however, is that it's not impossible to write a sparkling essay on an ordinary subject. A fresh, honest, and thoughtfully-written essay, regardless of its subject, is always welcome in college admissions offices.

DO . . .

✓ Answer the question that is asked.

✓ Choose a subject that you care about.

✓ Let your head and heart be your source of material.

✓ Think of at least three very good personal reasons for your choice.

✓ Try out more than one answer. Submit the one that you like best.

DON'T . . .

✗ Choose a topic merely to look good.

✗ Be self-conscious about your choice. Just tell the truth.

✗ Choose a subject that requires research. Let your experience guide you.

Answers That Worked

Sabrina S is the drum major of her school's marching band. She recalls a time when she thought that winning competitions was the band's only purpose. As a senior, she realizes that there's more to it than collecting trophies. The band has become an essential part of her life. "The school parking lot became my 'home' and the members of the band have become my 'family,'" she wrote.

Barbara B has been fascinated with space flight ever since second grade when the elementary school librarian introduced her to a science fiction book, *Matthew Looney, the Boy from the Moon*. In college Barbara expects to major in physics and then become an astronaut.

Luke J chose the word *family* as his favorite noun. To explain, he wrote a moving portrait of a close-knit family. Five times in the last ten years the family has moved. Luke's father works overseas for months at a time. Yet, Luke derives stability from his family, despite its fragmented lifestyle.

Robert B refuted the old adage, "You can't compare apples and oranges," by writing a tongue-in-cheek comparison of the two fruits. As a result, he wonders about the validity of other pieces of wisdom. He plans to research next "You can't tell a book by its cover" and "Absence makes the heart grow fonder."

Carl G, who has a deaf younger brother, wrote about *Dancing without Music—Deafness in America*, a book that persuaded him and his parents to introduce young Danny to other deaf people as a way to help the boy find an identity as a hearing-impaired person.

Gary K wrote about Steven, his mentally retarded brother. All his life, Gary has been Steven's fun committee, psychiatrist-at-home, and teacher. Gary wept recently after he found Steven eating pineapple from a can. It had taken Gary six weeks to teach Steven how to use a can opener.

Joanna L wrote that there's nothing better than hearing the expression "Time's up" in gym class. As she put it, "Gym has always been intimidating to me. It has convinced me that physically I am, and always will be, a clumsy oaf. . . . The smell of a gymnasium and the sight of orange mats stimulate feelings of terror and dread."

Ian R said he'd like to have dinner with Bill Gates. "I identify with him," Ian wrote. "On the outside, he looks like a schnook, the guy next door who gets bullied on the school bus. I've always been (and I'm proud to admit it) somewhat nerdy myself." Ian goes on to explain that he'd ask Bill Gates to divulge the secret of how a nerd can become one of the richest and most powerful men in America.

Marley E picked Alfred Lansing's *Endurance: Shackleton's Incredible Voyage* as a book that had special significance for him. Shackleton, an Antarctic explorer, survived with his crew for five months on a drifting ice pack in one of the most treacherous areas in the world. "The determination of the men to survive is awe-inspiring," wrote Marley. "They endured incredible suffering with superhuman courage. Their inspirational story made me aware as never before of the potential of humans to overcome physical and emotional hardship. As a result of reading this book, my opinion of humanity has taken a giant leap forward and strengthened my own resolve to succeed in life."

What Would You Like to Tell Us About Yourself?

Perhaps the toughest question is the one without a suggested topic:

> —We would welcome any comments you care to make about yourself.

—The essay is an important part of your application. It will help admissions officers gain a more complete picture of you. Use the essay to tell about yourself.

—If there is anything else you would like to tell us about you, please explain on an additional sheet.

—Please use this page to give us any information you think would be helpful to us as we consider your application.

—The purpose of this application is to help us learn about you.

—Is there additional information we should know that will help us to make an informed decision?

—To better understand you, what else should we know?

Without restrictions, you may literally send in anything. Starting from scratch, you can cook up a totally new piece of writing. Or you may submit a poem, a story, or a paper you've written for school or yourself. Applicants who have written for publications often send samples of their writing. If you include a previously written piece, don't just pull it from your files and throw it in the envelope. Carefully explain on a new cover page what it is and why you chose it.

In response to this question, one applicant to Ohio Wesleyan sent in a scrapbook of his experience as a congressional committee witness on children's health care, a matter that affected him personally. To the admissions committee, this was a compelling statement about his dedication and ability to advocate for something he believed, even at a relatively young age.

Although colleges say they want to know you better, you don't have to reveal an intimate secret about yourself. Applicants have sent in essays about child abuse, divorce, anorexia, surviving cancer—you name it. Essay readers are moved by human tragedy no more and no less than the rest of us, but they won't lower their admission standards because you have suffered. Rather, they look for applicants who can reflect on their hardships with wisdom and maturity. They're aware of human misery, but they look for more than the fact that you went through a bad experience. They want to know what you think about it now.

DO . . .

✓ Pick something important—something that matters to you.

✓ Consider explaining anything unusual that has influenced your school or home life.

✓ Use a style of writing that sounds like you.

✓ Write the sort of piece (for example, essay, poem, internal monologue) that you've written successfully in the past.

DON'T . . .

✗ Turn down the college's invitation to write more about yourself.

✗ Put on airs to try to impress the college. Be yourself.

✗ Repeat what you've written elsewhere on your application.

✗ Try to use a form or style of writing for the first time unless you have a record of successful writing experiments.

✗ Write the essay (or any other part of your application) the night before it's due.

Answers That Worked

Bonnie W asserted that writing the college essay helped her sort out her feelings about herself. She has finally accepted the fact that she is a nonconformist. "I used to run with the 'in' crowd," she wrote, "but now I don't give a damn. I can breathe."

Lillian S, a student of karate, wrote about how it feels to break a board with her bare hand. Writing about karate, she said, has heightened her concentration as she trains to earn a black belt.

Dave E reflected on violence in America. His thoughts had been triggered by a triple murder that had occurred a few weeks earlier in a neighboring town.

Kevin B wrote a funny piece on being a motorcycle enthusiast. On a recent trip to Massachusetts with the school band, his overnight host expected him to come equipped with a switchblade and chains. The folks in the Bay State seemed disappointed by his "normal" behavior and appearance.

Jenny J wrote a collection of fables, each concluding with a moral or maxim to illustrate a strongly held conviction. One story ended, "Be satisfied with who you are." Another, "Don't turn your back on anyone in pursuit of power."

Adam B wrote a piece detailing the first time he baked walnut tarts. Like an expectant father, he paced the kitchen floor, waiting for the oven bell to sound. At the gong, his whole family rushed in for a taste. The verdict? "Well, that night I retired with a grin on my face," wrote Adam.

Ray G, a high school baseball player, wrote a tongue-in-cheek analysis of his statistics. Last season he batted .300. He also got 600 on his math SAT. "Does that mean my math is twice as good as my hitting?" Ray asked. "I doubt that my math teacher would say so," he added.

Jodi F wrote about a family trip to Europe. Her parents were on the verge of separation, but during the tour of Italy, France, and Spain her mother and father made peace. "How odd," thought Jodi, "to save my home by leaving it."

Barry G wrote of waking in the middle of a hot summer night and going to the roof of his apartment building for some air. Peering at the lights below, he experienced a self-revelation. As an intelligent person, he realized that if he set his mind to it, he could do almost anything he wanted to with his life. Thinking of possibilities, he stayed on the roof until dawn.

Pamela M reviewed her dancing career since age four and concluded by stating, "Dancing has allowed me to express myself from within and to be, feel, and love who I am."

Martin S wrote about playing the piano. To show that he is a stellar pianist was not his point, however. Rather, he focused on the psychological differences he felt between playing for himself and playing for a public performance or a competition. "On my own," he wrote, "I don't have to control my mind so much. I can let intuitive hunches flow into my hands. A small inner voice speaks to me, allowing me to experience moments of real feeling or insight. Suddenly, highly-charged music far transcends the notes printed on the page."

Thinking of Ideas to Write About

If you're one of those blessed writers who explode with ideas for every assignment, read no further. You don't need this section. If, however, you routinely come back empty handed from topic searches, try some of these popular do-it-yourself techniques for spawning ideas:

1. If your essay due date is weeks or months away, start a journal today. Innumerable college essays have begun life as journal entries. From now on, record whatever catches your eye or tickles your brain. Anything! Since no one else will see what you write, literally everything is OK. Some of what you write may be silly and pointless, but not if you force yourself to tell the truth and only the truth.

   Frankly, your honest images and thoughts may lead to a dead end, but journal keepers often run into rich veins of ideas in their daily entries. After a few days, a journal begins to be a source book of information on you. When you need a topic for your college essay, you'll have a personal reference book at your fingertips. In its pages you may discover the stuff to write the essay of your life.

2. Try free-writing. That is, write nonstop for ten to fifteen minutes a day, paying no heed to grammar, spelling, or punctuation. Concentrate on telling the truth about whatever is on your mind that day. You'll be amazed at how rapidly ideas flow when you write unself-consciously and without preplanning. After free-writing you won't have a polished essay, or even a first draft, but you might have bagged one or two surprisingly fertile ideas.

3. Focus your free-writing. Once you have done some free-writing, reread what you've written. Circle any idea or phrase you like or that holds promise for an essay topic. Take one of the ideas that feels right, and free-write on that one. When you focus your free-writing, you accumulate possibilities on a topic. The human mind spits out thoughts so speedily that most of them vanish before they reach consciousness. In free-writing, though, you can preserve thoughts before they get away. Try focused free-writing again and again, until you've arrived at a satisfactory essay topic.

4. Like pulling out a stopper, making a list often starts the flow of ideas. A list of items, quickly jotted down, may bring to mind just the topic you're looking for. Writing down lists of influential people in your life or books you've read acts like a simple word-association exercise. As your mind makes connections, one name calls up memories of the next and the next. Anything and anyone can go on your list. At first, don't be particular. Later you can start to be discriminating as you narrow the choices for a possible essay topic.

5. On a very long sheet of paper—perhaps a roll of printer or art kraft paper—create a timeline of your life. Write down every event you can think of, whether you think it's important or not. Ask people whom you've known for a long time to suggest additional items for your time line. A perusal of the finished work may suggest lifelong themes, key events, and personal interests that can be turned into essay topics.

6. Talk to anyone who'll listen—a teacher or coach, a boss or a soulmate also in search of a topic. When you least expect it, one of you might just blurt out the very idea you've been looking for. Besides, when you solve a problem with someone else, you often get a bonus called synergism—the combined power of two heads working together, which usually exceeds the total power of two heads working separately.

4 COMPOSING YOUR ESSAY

You probably won't get out of high school without writing some sort of essay on *Macbeth,* or if not *Macbeth,* then on the Great Depression or protein synthesis. By this time in your life, in fact, you've probably written enough essays to fill a large book. When writing those essays, perhaps you sat down, spilled your thoughts onto the computer screen, printed it out, and handed in your paper. Maybe you wrote a rough draft and went back later to rephrase and cut and paste your ideas. Possibly, you thought out ahead of time what you wanted to say and prepared a list of ideas or an outline. Maybe you used a combination of methods, varying them from time to time according to the importance of the essay.

Everyone who writes uses a process of some kind. Some processes seem to work better than others. The variations are endless, however, and the actual process you use is as personal and unique as your fingerprints. Since it is personal, let me step out of my role as writing instructor for a moment and describe the process I used to write this chapter so far.

Before I even turned my computer on, I had a general idea of what I wanted to say: namely, that anyone facing an essay question on a college application has already had plenty of writing experience and that the same process a person used to write essays in school can be used to write an essay for college. Furthermore, I wanted to assure the

> The process you use to write is as personal and unique as your fingerprints.

reader that no single process is better than any other, as long as it works. With those thoughts floating around in my head, I started to write, hoping that one idea would flow smoothly into the next. I also hoped that extraneous ideas wouldn't lead me away from what I had in mind, something that frequently happens when I write.

Fairly rapidly for me, because I'm usually a very slow writer, I typed the first two paragraphs. Then I reread them. Luckily, they seemed to stick to the topic and they more or less expressed my thoughts. I wasn't altogether happy with my opening sentence, however, which originally read, "By this time in your life you must have written a ream of essays." I thought that some of my readers wouldn't know the word *ream,* so I changed the sentence to one that would surely evoke an image of a lot of pages: "By this time in your life you must have written enough essays to fill a large book."

A moment later, however, I decided that even that sentence wasn't right for an opening. I needed an idea that hit closer to my readers' experience. So I inserted two new sentences, turning my original first sentence into the third. Still later, I added the phrase "in fact" to that sentence, intending to bind the thoughts in the first three sentences more closely to each other.

As you see, I like to write a few paragraphs as quickly as I can, then return to them before going on. I don't always do that, however. Sometimes I write more, sometimes less, before doubling back to rewrite and edit. Other writers work differently, and so, no doubt, do you.

If you compare my original opening paragraphs, reproduced below, with the printed version at the start of this chapter, you'll discover several more changes, each intended to make the writing clearer and more interesting. All the while, I kept thinking of you, my reader. I figured that if you are going to spend time reading my words, the least I could do is make the time worth your while. I also wanted to make you feel compelled to read on. If your cell phone rang while you were reading, I was hoping you'd be annoyed at the interruption.

> By this time in your life you must have written a ream of essays. In fourth grade, remember writing about "My Trip to Disney World"? More recently, perhaps, you wrote about irony in *Macbeth* or Chinese immigration to the United States. When you wrote those essays, you probably used a technique that seemed right for you. Perhaps you just sat down, spilled your thoughts onto the page, went back later, and reorganized and rephrased your ideas over and over. You may have thought out what you wanted to say ahead of time and prepared some sort of list or outline of your ideas to guide you as you wrote. You may have used a combination of methods.

> Everyone who writes anything uses a process of some kind. Some processes seem to work better than others for certain writers. The variations are endless, however, and the actual process you use is personal and as unique to you as your fingerprints. Since it is so personal, let me step down from my post as giver of information about essay writing for a moment and describe the process I used to write this chapter so far.

Thinking About the Reader

You and I have made a kind of agreement. Simply by reading these words, you have agreed to let me enter your life. Thanks. My end of the bargain is harder. I have to keep writing until I'm finished, but you can stop reading at any time.

I don't want you to stop, however. So as I write, I try everything I can to hold your interest, to keep your mind and eyes fastened to these words. That's a tough assignment. Since you're a stranger to me, I don't know what you'll understand or what will grab you. I have to keep guessing. Even if my guess is wrong, I can't stop, can't go back and try again. If you shut this book right now, I'll never know it. No physical force in the universe is strong enough to keep one small muscle in your head from shifting your eyes away from this page. Only the compelling power of my words, along with some lucky guesswork, can do it.

As a writer of a college essay, you face a challenge similar to mine, except that you can be pretty sure your reader will stick with you to the last word. Because you have a reasonable guarantee of an audience doesn't make the job of writing any easier, however. You're still obliged to give the readers something they want to read. Writing the essay is a lot like giving a gift to a friend. You think about what your friend would like, you try to please, you choose carefully and you present the gift as stylishly as you can. If all goes well, you get a reward for your effort.

> Writing an essay is a lot like giving a gift to a friend. You try to please.

But, first, it's work.

Warming Up

Once you know the questions on your application, you're likely to start thinking about what to write. As you reach into your background to search for a subject, don't lose heart if at first you come up empty-handed. You may need a warming-up period to help you find a subject and to prime you for the vigorous mental work ahead. In fact, the ultimate quality of your essay may depend in part on your warm-ups.

For most students, the high school years rush by like a raging river. It's hard to stop and step back a moment to reflect on your life, on how far you've come and where you'd like to go. Now, on the verge of applying to college, is the right time for you to try.

Start with a personal inventory. The key word is *personal*—for your eyes only. Think of who you are and how you got that way. You might begin, for example, simply by making a list of adjectives that describe what you like about yourself. Then make another list of what you dislike. Don't worry if the second list is longer than the first—most people are pretty hard on themselves. Study these lists for patterns, inconsistencies, and unusual combinations. For instance, Gina S, whose list appears below, considers herself both "generous to others" and "self-centered." Is Gina contradicting herself? Is she being untruthful? Does she change from time to time? Since the list is personal, no one but Gina needs to know.

Gina's Personal Inventory

What I like about myself	*What I dislike*
loyal to my friends	my nose
idealistic	short temper
trusting	uncomfortable with
prompt in replying to	strangers
instant messages	need a lot of sleep
determined to succeed	living in the past
mysterious	impulsive
ambitious	lack of athletic talent
competitive	can't carry a tune
generous to others	gluttonish
insightful about myself	envious of friends
sensitive to others' feelings	(sometimes)
good listener	overconsiderate of
good memory	others (sometimes)
energetic	math and heavy metal
flirtatious	often late for appoint-
skillful as a blogger	ments
	self-centered
	stubborn
	basically shy
	indecisive

Once you complete a list, rank the qualities in order of importance. Which quality would you be most reluctant to give up?
Which would you give up first? Which are you proudest of? Which
would you most like to change? A compilation of answers to such
questions identify your interests and, to a degree, define your values and describe your personality.

Most items on your own personal inventory will differ from
Gina's. Yet, it shouldn't surprise you to find some similarities.
Although no item may immediately strike you as the focus of a distinctive essay, a few imaginative connections could lead you directly
to a suitable subject. Notice how Gina might have developed several
possible subjects from her inventory:

> Gina claims to be "competitive," but she also "lacks athletic
> talent." Her competitive nature, therefore, may emerge in the
> classroom instead of the gym. Perhaps she competes to win
> awards as the best reader, writer or mathematician. She may
> compete for recognition on the job or at home. Regardless of
> the place, Gina's need to excel could be the focus of her essay.
>
> Gina says she's a "glutton," presumably for food. Since a
> college doesn't necessarily need to know that, Gina could
> turn gluttony into a metaphor and focus her essay on being
> a glutton for success. Perhaps she derives satisfaction from
> being a successful student, friend or member of a particular
> group.
>
> Gina also says she's "impulsive." In a way, her "short tem-
> per" confirms that she occasionally rushes into things. On the
> other hand, she might point out that her impulsiveness gives
> her an urge to help anyone in need. Her essay might focus on
> an incident that demonstrates her unusual generosity. A brief
> discussion about becoming a social worker someday would
> add a fitting conclusion to her essay.

Ultimately, Gina found her subject in an incident that would
not have occurred unless she truly had a "good memory." This
excerpt from her essay tells what happened:

> I had just come from the elephant house at the zoo when I
> spotted Bucky, my old swimming counselor at Camp
> Merriwood. It was six years since I saw him last. I remem-
> bered him only in a Princeton tee shirt and a swimsuit and
> never imagined that he even owned long pants and a parka,
> but I recognized his face instantly. I called out his name and
> introduced myself.

He looked at me and said, "Oh, I remember you, Gina," but I knew he was just being polite. To him I could have been Jenny, Margie, Eva, Ruthie, Lilah, Lucy, or any one of the dozens of squealing ten-year-old girls at camp that summer.

We talked a little while about people and events at camp. No, he didn't really remember the kids on my relay team. Well yes, he only had a faint memory of the swim meet we won against Camp Harding, in which I won two races.

"What are you up to now?" he asked. When I told him I was looking for a summer job, he said his company sometimes hired high school students in the summer and that I should apply.

Gina landed a summer job in Bucky's firm doing something called "customer relations," a glamorous term for helping to keep the files straight. Gina observed in her essay, though, that she was glad to be working at all. Then she added:

I got the job as a result of having a good memory. Since then I have become more interested in memory and how it works. I have read some books on the subject and have learned some ways to improve my own memory. In less than a minute I can now memorize ten vocabulary words or the names of ten people I never met before. Elephants are not supposed to forget, which may or may not be true. However, I wonder if remembering Bucky was related to my visit to the elephants in the zoo.

Gina launched her essay with a short anecdote meant to illustrate her good memory. For every quality you list on a personal inventory, try also to think of evidence that proves that you are indeed what you claim to be. A single example is all it takes to get an essay underway.

Another place to locate essay subjects is in your answers to a set of questions such as these:

—What are you good at?
—What are you trying to get better at?
—What has been your greatest success? Your greatest failure?
—What three words would you like engraved on your tombstone?
—What is your strongest conviction? Would you die for it?
—What would you do with a million dollars?

—If the world were to end a year from today, how would you spend your remaining time?

Thoughtful answers to often whimsical questions may trigger any number of essay possibilities. As you toss ideas back and forth in your head, keep your distance from stock responses—those that will lump you with the crowd. Walk around for a few days letting yourself think about what makes you unique. Tell someone what's on your mind. Keep a notebook in your pocket, because a great thought may hit you at any time. Keep pen and pad by your bed to record a four-in-the-morning inspiration. Do some free-writing. Think hard about what you want your readers to think of you. In short, do something to jump-start your writing muscles.

Some people call this part of the process "prewriting." You might call it getting yourself "psyched." Whatever the name, it's the time you spend messing with possibilities and tuning up to write. It may even include finding a quiet, uncluttered place to work without distractions. It involves laying aside many hours of time for solitary, unhurried work.

> Prewriting may include finding a quiet place for hours of solitary, unhurried work.

Warm-up time should also include a search for the point, or focus, of your essay. Identifying a subject isn't enough. Now you must focus on what you'll say about the subject. The sharper your focus, the better. You can't expect to include everything in a 250- to 500-word essay.

Maybe the surest way to narrow your subject is to begin writing. If your essay seems dull and disappointing after a couple of paragraphs, you're probably being too vague, too impersonal, or both. Keep going, for you may discover the point of your essay at any time. Be prepared, however, to recognize that you may occasionally write yourself into a dead end. Not every subject works. If you find yourself blocked on all sides, you have no choice but to grit your teeth, turn to another topic, and start over.

If you end up dry, even after several attempts, you might try this twenty-question technique for unlocking ideas. Write your subject at the top of a page. Then ask twenty questions about the subject, leaving plenty of space for writing answers. Linda W, for example, knew she wanted to write an essay on dancing, but she didn't know what to say about it. At first she wrote, "During the last eight years dancing has provided me with great satisfaction." Because every devoted ballerina feels exactly the same way, however, Linda quickly realized that her idea was an out-and-out bore. So Linda started asking and answering questions like these:

> What kind of dancing do I like the most?

> When did I first fall in love with dancing?

> Why doesn't everybody dance?

> What would my life be like without dancing?

> Who has been important to me in my dancing? Why?

> If I could not dance, what art form would I use to express myself?

> What am I giving up or sacrificing by devoting so much time to dance?

> How good a dancer am I? How can I find out?

The first questions were easy. When the questions grew hard, both to ask and to answer, Linda had begun to dig deeply into her topic. In figuring out answers, she finally discovered an original point to make in her essay:

> To me, dancing is the most dynamic and personal of the arts. Pictures and sculptures are displayed in museums. Poems and stories are hidden in books. To make music you play someone else's notes on an instrument made by another person. But dancing, ah, dancing, is like life itself.

Where Linda crossed over from prewriting to actually composing her first draft is hard to say, nor is it critical to know. What counts is that she found a topic, narrowed its focus, and stated a compelling thesis for an essay.

Writing the Essay

By the time some writers begin to compose their essays they more or less know that they'll reach their destination using the famous five-paragraph essay formula. Other writers will start more tentatively, knowing their general direction but not finding the specific route until they get there.

Neither method is better than the other, for much depends on the subject matter and intent of the writer. The first method follows a simple, clear-cut formula, which may not win a prize for originality but can help to turn a muddle of ideas into a model of clarity. It has a beginning, a middle, and an end.

The *formula* is simply an all-purpose plan for arranging ideas into a clear, easy-to-follow order. You have probably used it in school for answering a test question, analyzing a poem or reporting lab work. You can call on it anytime you need to set ideas in order. Its greatest virtue is clarity. Each part has its place and purpose.

The formula

Introduction

Body
{ Point 1
  Point 2
  Point 3

Conclusion

In reality, however, writers rarely follow the *formula*. In fact, you may never see a formula essay in print. Yet a majority of college essays, even those that take circuitous paths between the beginning and end, adhere to some sort of three-step organization. In the *introduction,* writers lay out their plans for the essay. In the *body* they develop their ideas, and in the *conclusion* they leave the reader with a thought to remember. Since all writers differ, however, you find endless variations within each step, as you're about to see.

Introductions: Hooking the Reader

Use the introduction to let readers know what they're in for. Don't, however, make a formal announcement of your plan: "This essay is about poverty in Manhattan." Just state your point. The reader will recognize the topic soon enough, even without a separate statement of your intention. Maria G, for example, began her essay this way: "Working one weekend a month in Mother Theresa's Soup Kitchen on the lower East Side with the St. Augustine Teen Club has changed my life." This opening promises the reader an account of Maria's weekends in the slums and what the experience has meant to her. It also sets the essay's boundaries. Maria can't include everything about dismal conditions in lower Manhattan. Instead, she'll concentrate on her own experience there, and no more.

> The best essays begin with a "hook" to catch the reader's interest.

The best essays usually begin with something catchy, something to lure the reader into the piece. Basically, it's a hook—a phrase, sentence, or idea that will grab readers' interest so completely that they'll keep on reading almost in spite of themselves. Once you've hooked your readers, you can lead them anywhere.

Hooks must be very sharp, very clean. They must surprise, inform, or tickle the reader in an instant. A dull hook just won't do. Here are a few samples of each:

DULL HOOK

My difficulty in dealing with my feelings probably all started when my parents' marriage started breaking up.

SHARPER HOOK

The first thing I remember is my parents arguing in the next room while I was trying to sleep.

The sharper hook is vivid. It creates a compelling image of a child in the dark, attempting to block out the sounds of his parents' shouting. It also provokes curiosity. The reader wants to know more.

DULL HOOK

The book, *Divine Comedy,* is a serious work of literature, written by Dante several centuries ago.

SHARPER HOOK

Dante's *Divine Comedy,* despite its title, is not a funny book.

The second hook contains a small surprise for the reader. No one who knows Dante's work about the author's travels through Hell, would think of it as humorous. Yet, a student coming to the title for the first time might expect to be amused. The mistake is worth a chuckle—but only if you're familiar with the book.

DULL HOOK

Among my various extracurricular commitments, music has been the most enduring.

SHARPER HOOK

I have tried to immerse myself in music.

In the sharper hook, the terse declaration of the writer's commitment to music makes the point quickly. As the reader, you know instantly that music is the topic. Moreover, the repetition of the "m" sound has a certain appeal.

Naturally, your essay's opening ought to be appropriate to your topic and tone. A serious discussion of Mother Theresa's Soup Kitchen probably shouldn't begin with an irreverent story about a nun. Beware also of any introduction that's too cute or precious. Be thoughtful and clever, yes; obnoxious, no. If you quickly want to lure your reader into your essay, consider any of these five common methods:

> Your opening should be appropriate to your topic and tone.

1. Start with an incident, real or invented, that leads the reader gracefully to the point of your essay.

   > "How about 'John Henry' in A?"
   > The banjo player kicks off the tune with a solid lead and is joined by the other field pickers in a couple of seconds. Having sung the first verse and chorus, I strum along on the guitar and let my mind wander. How incongruous for me, a product of upper-middle-class suburbia, to be standing in the middle of a grassy field picking bluegrass and old-timey music until dawn.
   > —Steve M

2. State a provocative idea in an ordinary way or an ordinary idea in a provocative way. Either will spark the reader's interest.

   > If you've never been six feet seven inches tall like me, you probably don't know what it's like up here. Everybody is a

comedian when they meet you. They call you "Beanpole," or ask, "How's the weather up there?" or tell you to "Watch out for low-flying planes!" Not only that, they expect you to play basketball, have bumps on your head from doorways, and know things that shorties don't.

—Andy S

3. Use a quotation—not necessarily a famous one. Shakespeare's or your grandmother's will do, as long as it relates to the topic of your essay.

True ease in writing comes from art, not chance,
as those move easiest who have learn'd to dance.
—Alexander Pope,
An Essay on Criticism

It took me eight years to understand Pope's message. I know now that he should have said, "True ease in dance comes from wonderful, frustrating, exciting, tedious, time-consuming, strenuous, and sweaty work, not chance." That may not sound as good, but it's as true.

—Lisa B

4. Knock down a commonly held assumption or define a word in a new and surprising way.

No doubt you've heard that Latin is a dead language. Wrong! Latin is alive and well and living inside my head, thanks to a wonderful teacher who emphasized the culture, not the conjugations, in the language.

—Alicia G

5. Ask an interesting question or two, which you will answer in your essay.

"Tell me, in God's name, why you, Terry D, want to become an English teacher!"

"Because . . . because I want to teach," I stammered. I bent my head, hoping my answers would satisfy him and defuse the unbearable tension that stalked about me.

"Come, Terry, that's not the reason; there's more to it than what you've said. Now why do you want to teach? Is it the

kids? The classroom? Power? What force within yourself
causes you to associate English and teaching?"

—Teresa D

In any collection of good essays you'd no doubt find other
examples of catchy openings. Whatever your opening, however, it
must fit your writing style and personality. Work hard at getting it
right, but at the same time, not too hard. An opening that seems
forced may irk your reader, and one that comprises, say, more than
a quarter of your essay is way too long.

If you can't find a suitable opening when you begin to write
your essay, don't put off writing the rest. As you write the body of
the essay, a bright idea may hit you. Some writers begin by writing three paragraphs, fully expecting to throw away the first two.
They need at least two paragraphs to hit their stride and to rid
their minds of useless ideas. By the time they've reached paragraph three, they've figured out the point of their essays. Only
then do they turn to writing a hook. You might try that. If your
"throwaway" paragraphs contain ideas you can't live without, re-
cycle them later in your essay.

The Body: Putting the Pieces Together

To build a house you must start on the ground. On your foundation
you construct a frame, then add walls, a roof, a satellite dish and
you're done! The builder must follow this order or the house will
crumble.

Order is important to the writer, too. What should come first?
Second? Third? In most writing the best order is the clearest order,
the arrangement your reader can follow with the least effort.

Just as a highway map shows several routes from one town to
another, there is no single way to get from the beginning of a piece
of writing to the end. The route you take depends on the purpose
of the trip. The order of ideas in the body of your essay will vary
according to what you want to do to your reader. Whether you
want to shock, sadden, inspire, inform, or entertain the reader,
each purpose will have its own best order. In storytelling, the
events are often placed in the sequence in which they occur. To
explain a childhood memory or define who you are, to stand up for
gay rights or describe a poignant moment—each may take some
other particular arrangement. No one plan is superior to another,
provided you have a valid reason for using it.

The plan that fails is the aimless one, the one in which ideas
are arranged solely on the basis of the order in which they popped

> To hold the reader's interest, work toward your best point, not away from it.

into your head. To guard against aim-lessness, rank your ideas in order of importance either before you start or while you're writing drafts. Although your first idea may turn out to be your best, you probably should save it for later in your essay. Giving it away at the start is self-defeating. To hold your reader's interest, it's better to work toward your best point, not away from it. If you have, say, three good points to make, save your zinger for last. Launch your essay with your second best, and tuck your least favorite between the other two.

A body consisting of three sections may be just about right, although no hard-and-fast rule says so. Why *three*? Mainly because three is a number that seems to work. When you can make three statements about a subject, you probably know what you're talking about. One is too simple, and two is still pretty shallow, but three seems thoughtful. Psychologically, three also creates a sense of wholeness, like the beginning, middle, and end of a story. Each point doesn't necessarily receive equal treatment. You might manage one point with a single paragraph, but the others may get more. Each point has to be distinctive: Your third point mustn't be a rerun of the first or second.

It shouldn't be difficult to break the main point of most essays into at least three secondary points, regardless of their topic or form. A narrative essay, for example, naturally breaks into a beginning, middle, and end. A process is likely to have at least three steps, some of which may be broken into substeps. In an essay of comparison and contrast, you ought to be able to find at least three similarities and differences to write about. A similar division into thirds applies to essays of cause and effect, definition and description, and certainly to essays of argumentation.

Turn back to the sample essays in Chapter 2. Each of the successful pieces follows the three-part pattern. In rough outline, they look like this:

Chandra's essay (page 33)

Subject: The struggles within me

Point 1:   What do I stand for?

Point 2:   What should I do with my life?

Point 3:   How can I communicate with others?

Angela's essay (page 35)

Subject:	My field hockey career
Point 1:	Starting out in ninth grade—a social activity
Point 2:	In tenth and eleventh grade—fun and dedication
Point 3:	Becoming a champion—a serious commitment

Eric's essay (page 37)

Subject:	Joint custody
Point 1:	Description of my weekly ordeal
Point 2:	My relationship with my mother and father
Point 3:	How joint custody has changed me

Only Joyce's essay (page 31) defies analysis into three sections. In fact, the piece fails for the very reason that Joyce tried to make more than half a dozen different points. Each point remains undeveloped, and in the end the essay is little more than a list of Joyce's interests and activities.

Transitions and Paragraphs: Taking Readers by the Hand

Readers need to be led. As you write, think of readers as tourists and your essay as a trip they take from one place to another. You are their guide, their travel agent.

After you've told them where they're going (the introduction), now and then remind them (in the body of the essay) where they're headed. In long essays readers need more reminders than in short ones. To keep readers well informed, you don't have to repeat what you've written, but rather plant key ideas, slightly rephrased, as milestones along the way. (The sentence you just read contains just such a marker. The phrase *"To keep a reader well informed"* prompts you to keep in mind the topic being discussed—that is, helping readers find their way.) Watch out for detours, for you may lose your readers if you step too far outside the path you laid out at the start. (The sentence you just read is a detour. Yes, it's related to the topic but it steers the discussion away from guiding readers through an essay.)

Help readers along, too, by choosing words that set up relationships between one idea and the next. This can be done with such words as *this,* which, for example, ties the sentence you are now reading to the previous one. The English language supplies many words and phrases for tying sentences and ideas together, among them:

also	on the other hand	still
too	consequently	another
further	therefore	finally
in addition	although	in the first place
similarly	moreover	regardless
as a result	nevertheless	on the contrary
however	now	better still
for instance	this	yet

Each time you link one sentence to another with a transitional word or phrase, you help to clear a path for readers through your writing. Without such help, or when every sentence stands unconnected to the next, readers may end up hopelessly lost, like travelers going down roads without signposts or markers.

Links between sentences lend a hand to writers, too. They help writers stick to the topic. Ideas that don't connect clearly with others should be moved or thrown out.

The inventor of the paragraph also figured out a simple way to mark the path through a piece of writing. The paragraph indentation is a signal to readers to get ready for a change in thought or idea, somewhat like the directional blinker telling other drivers that you're about to turn.

Yet not every new paragraph signals a drastic change. The writer may simply want to move the essay ahead one step at a time, and paragraphs illuminate each step.

Some paragraphs spring directly from those that came before. Like infants, they can't stand alone. The paragraph before this one, for example, is linked to the previous one by the connecting word *yet.* The connection has cued you to get ready for a contrasting thought, but it also reminded you that the two paragraphs are related.

Abrupt starts are best from time to time. Suddenness will surprise and keep readers alert. Connecting words will dilute the impact of the surprise. Be wary of a string of abrupt starts, however, because too many quick shifts may annoy more than surprise.

Paragraphs let your readers skip rapidly through your work, particularly when each first or last sentence summarizes the rest of the paragraph. Readers may then focus on paragraph openings and closings and skip what's in between. Readers in a hurry will appreciate that, but you can force readers to linger a while by varying the location of the most important idea in each paragraph.

Whether your readers skim the paragraphs or slog doggedly through every word, they need to find sentences now and then that, like landmarks, help them to know where they are. Such guiding sentences differ from others because they define the paragraph's main topic; hence the name *topic sentence.*

Most, but not all, paragraphs contain topic sentences. The topic of some paragraphs is so obvious that to state it would be redundant. Then, too, groups of paragraphs can be so closely knit that one topic sentence states the most important idea for all of them.

No rule governs every possible use of a topic sentence. A sense of what readers need in order to understand your meaning must guide you. Consider your readers absent-minded wanderers. Since they tend to lose their way, remind them often about where they are. Let the topic sentences lead. If in doubt, grasp their hands too firmly rather than too loosely. Follow the principle that if there is any way to misunderstand or misinterpret your words, readers are bound to find it.

> Consider your readers absent-minded wanderers. Remind them often where they are.

The Conclusion: Giving a Farewell Gift

When you reach the end of your essay, you can stop writing and be done with it. Or, you can present your reader with a little something to remember you by, a *gift*—an idea to think about, a line to chuckle over, a memorable phrase or quotation. Whatever you give, the farewell gift must fit the content, style, and mood of your essay.

> Send your readers off feeling glad that they stayed with you to the end.

Some writers think that endings are more important than beginnings. After all, by the time readers arrive at the conclusion, your introduction may have already begun to fade from memory.

Making a reference to the opening reminds readers of the essay's purpose. It also creates a sense of wholeness. A well-phrased ending will stick with readers and influence their feelings about your essay and, of course, about its writer. Therefore, choose a farewell gift thoughtfully. Be particular. Send your readers off feeling good or laughing, weeping, angry, thoughtful, or thankful, but above all, glad that they stayed with your essay to the end.

A conclusion that's too pat or common will leave readers with the impression that you were too cheap to give the best gift you could, or that you chose your gift in haste. Stay away especially from bargain-basement gifts like these:

> The challenges I faced will help me in college and in the future. (from an essay on a significant experience)

> Then I woke up and saw that it was all a dream. (from an essay about talking with a famous person in history)

> I'd recommend this book to anyone who likes good psychological or murder stories. (from an essay about *Crime and Punishment,* an influential book in the writer's life)

> In conclusion, if I can be half as successful as my aunt, I will have fulfilled myself as an individual. (from an influential person essay)

Such trite endings suggest that the writers couldn't think of anything original to say or that they just wanted to get their essays over with. Either way, a stale conclusion can spoil a good essay.

Readers will appreciate almost any gift you give them, provided you've put some thought into your choice. When writing the ending, let your instinct guide you. You've read enough stories and plays and have heard enough songs to know what endings sound like, what lends a sense of completeness to a creative piece of work. For example, when you tell readers how an unresolved issue was settled, or when you speculate on what might occur in the future, readers sense that an ending is at hand.

Even commonly used endings can be turned into stylish gifts, as these samples show:

1. Have some fun with your ending. A reader may remember your sense of humor long after forgetting other details about you.

SUBJECT

Elizabeth H, an active member of many groups, treasures the hours she has for herself.

GIFT
___

Thoreau's remark, "I love to be alone," might well be my senior quote. In spite of the incessant plea of AT and T to "reach out and touch someone," there are some of us who would prefer to remain untouched. I am one of them.

SUBJECT
___

Debbie B's lifelong competition with her sister Michelle ended when Michelle left for college.

GIFT
___

. . . I stepped right into my sister's shoes (figuratively, not literally—because Michelle has a size five compared to my seven and a half). I think that my brain would become seriously warped if my feet were that squished.

2. End with an apt quotation, drawn either from the essay itself or from elsewhere.

SUBJECT
___

Craig S had to find safe shelter during a wilderness adventure.

GIFT
___

At that point I knew by instinct, "This is the place."

SUBJECT
___

Frank F had a part-time job in a hotel kitchen when a terrible fire broke out.

GIFT
___

To this day, whenever I smell food garbage, I hear the words, "Fire! Fire! Fire!" and the clang of fire bells.

3. Finish with a clear restatement of your essay's main point, using new words. Add a short tag line, perhaps.

SUBJECT

Carol B tells how she changed between ninth and eleventh grades.

GIFT

The main difference in me is that now I like myself. I could be friends with someone like me.

SUBJECT

Ian B learned about himself while reading Moss Hart's autobiography, *Act One*.

GIFT

There are no limits to the human spirit, no obstacles large enough to impede the attainment of a dream, provided that one's resolve and determination are equal to all the discouraging effects of failure. Further, there is no sin in initial failure. That's what I keep telling myself.

4. Bring the reader up to date or project him into the future.

SUBJECT

Ellen G tells of an old woman she met while working as a volunteer in a nursing home.

GIFT

I still visit Mrs. Thurnauer. Some weeks she is more vibrant than others. Even on her bad days I see her intelligence and courage. And even if on a certain day her hair is not combed back as smoothly as when I first met her, she still reminds me that growing old is not always a desperate process in which all pride and hope are lost.

SUBJECT

Jonathan M hopes to become a well-known (and rich) artist.

GIFT

Someday, collectors and museums may want to hang my paintings on their walls. I am always hopeful. Nevertheless, I am playing the lottery this week. The jackpot is $20 million and the odds of winning are only one in three million. I hope the probability is more favorable in the art world.

Above all, avoid the summary ending. Trust your reader to remember the substance of your one- or two-page essay. To say everything again is not only pointless, it borders on being an insult to the reader's intelligence. Your essay isn't a textbook. A chapter review isn't necessary.

Some essays don't need an extended conclusion. When they're over, they're over. Even a short conclusion is better than none at all, however. At the end, readers should feel that they've arrived somewhere. In a sense, every well-planned essay prepares readers for arrival at a certain destination. The introduction tells readers approximately where they're going. En route, a series of ideas propels them toward the conclusion. At the end they're welcomed with a thoughtful gift. When they get to the last word, you don't want readers to say, "Oh, now I see what you've been driving at."

5 REWRITING AND EDITING

This could be the hardest part of writing an essay. You've invested a lot of yourself in the work by this time. You won't want to go back now and start changing things. Who can blame you? Try, however, to resist the impulse to rest. It's not time, yet.

> Being tough on yourself is a courtesy to your readers.

Perhaps you're willing to alter a word here and there, check the spelling, relocate a comma or two, and repair a bit of broken-down grammar, but that's proofreading, not rewriting—and it's definitely not enough right now. Proofreading requires skills, but rewriting takes courage. It's painful work, for you may end up discarding large chunks of your essay and rewriting parts you've already rewritten. After you've struggled to get a paragraph just right, it's hard to give it up. Be brave. The next one you write may be even better.

Having Another Look

The root of revision is the word *vision,* that is, sight or perception. When revising, you *look again* to see whether you have said what you intended, and arranged your ideas in the best possible order. If you perceive a flaw or weakness, then revise—that is, *rewrite.* Read your essay ten, maybe twenty, times. During each reading, inspect it with a different set of lenses. Read it often for overall impression, but also to check it for each of these qualities:

- —*Accuracy.* Have you answered the question on the application?
- —*Purpose.* What do you want the reader to think of you after reading the essay? Have you portrayed yourself accurately? Does the essay sound like you?
- —*Focus.* Have you limited the subject enough to cover it well in a fairly short essay?
- —*Main idea.* What is the message you want to leave in the reader's mind?

—*Unity.* Do you stick to the point from beginning to end? Have you tied ideas together?

—*Organization.* Does your introduction draw readers into the essay? Can you explain the order of ideas in the body of your essay? What does your ending add to the essay?

—*Development.* What is the main point of each paragraph? What does each paragraph contribute to the whole? Have you said enough in each paragraph?

Being tough on yourself is a courtesy to your readers. College admissions officials have plenty to do. You'll spare them extra work by doing all you can to make your writing clear. Readers crave clarity. They want to understand what you say. They won't do your thinking for you. Don't assume, "They'll know what I mean." Tell them *exactly* what you mean. By doing so, you'll improve not only the essay but also your chances of being accepted.

As you rewrite, deprive the readers of every possible chance to stretch, garble, or misconstrue your meaning. Here are some methods you might try:

—*Read your essay aloud. Your ear is a good instrument for detecting words that don't sound right.*

—*Let someone read your essay aloud to you. Listen carefully, and watch his or her face for telltale signs of confusion or doubt.*

—*Let your essay cool for a while—a few hours, a day or so. When you come back, try to read it with the eyes of a stranger.*

The more rewriting you do, the better your essay is likely to be. On the other hand, you could write yourself right out of the essay. Too much painstaking revision may deprive the essay of its personality. The trick is to rewrite repeatedly but to make the words sound natural and spontaneous. Writers work for a long time to perfect the technique.

Finding Your "Voice"

In almost every essay that you're likely to write for a college, a natural, conversational style is appropriate. Since the essay should be personal, the language should sound like you—that is, like a thoughtful and well-spoken high school senior. When you use the pretentious language of a senator, the formal words of a legal document, or the slick style of, say, a TV commercial, you're going to sound like a senator, a lawyer, or a copywriter, not like an intelligent teenager applying to college.

So don't try to imitate anyone. Just let your genuine voice ring out. But don't confuse your "genuine voice" with everyday teen-talk or with an I.M. style of writing. It's not smart to cram your essay full of half-formed sentences, trendy usages, or pop phrases. Rather, consider the voice in your essay as the grammatically correct casual speech of someone who speaks well. As a rule, steer clear of writing anything that most students would feel uncomfortable saying aloud at a school board meeting or in a friendly conversation with a college interviewer.

> Don't imitate. Just let your genuine voice ring out.

Question: Can you find Becky's genuine voice in this passage?

> I desire so fervently to attend Amherst because I believe it is the only school that will enable me to explore my intellectual capabilities, heighten my perception of knowledge and gain a greater insight into myself and a greater understanding of others, in an atmosphere of united support for the individual.

No doubt, Becky wants Amherst, but she sounds more like a candidate for public office than a candidate for college. She conceals herself behind high-blown language that may sound important and profound but says very little—very little that's *clear,* at any rate. Contrast this with a passage from Lisa's essay about why she chose Wesleyan:

> During my visit in October, I had a good feeling about the academic life on the campus. It offers so much. I didn't want to go home and back to high school. Everyone I talked to in the dorm seemed happy about being in college there. If I am accepted, I'm sure that I will be bitten by the same bug of enthusiasm.

The voice you hear in Lisa's essay belongs to a genuine person. As she talks, you could be sitting next to her on the bus. Although informal, the writing is controlled.

You hear another kind of voice in this excerpt from the opening of Alec's essay for Columbia:

> You ask me to write an essay about myself. Eh? What can I say? Could Napoleon have written an essay about himself? Oh, what the hell, why not give it a crack, eh what?
>
> When I indulge in one of my favorite activities, thinking about myself, the word *unique* kicks around the old noggin. . . .

Alec sounds like a smart aleck. You'd never guess that he's a deep and discerning thinker. Later in the piece, however, he stops babbling and finds a more honest voice. Breezy it is, but no longer obnoxious:

> Enough about my intellectual musings (and what amusing musings they are). Another field of interest I cultivated in lieu of physical activity was acting. In the eight years that I have acted professionally, having appeared off Broadway and on a CBS movie of the week, I have basically developed into a character actor. However, I have been working on playing more natural parts lately, and even though I still play character parts, they have become less caricatured and more natural.
>
> Although I intend to pursue acting as a career, I don't intend to major in it. For two reasons: (1) I have other scholarly interests, and (2) I'm a klutz and could never wait on tables to support myself, so I hope to teach instead.

You can check your writing voice by having a friend hand your essay to someone who doesn't know you. If a stranger can describe you accurately after reading your work, you can safely say that you've been faithful to yourself.

Editing for Clarity

You probably started editing your essay soon after composing the first few lines. That is, you changed and reworded sentences to make certain they said what you wanted them to say. As you continue, regard every word and phrase as a potential threat to the clarity of your writing. Ask yourself repeatedly: Is this the clearest word for me to use here? Are these words arranged in the clearest order?

Plain Words

To write clearly, use plain words. Never use a complex word because it sounds good or it makes you seem more mature. A college essay is not the place to show off your vocabulary. Use a so-called SAT word only when necessary—that is, when it's the only word that will add something to the essay's tone and meaning, which you'll lose by using a common word. Keep that thesaurus on the shelf unless you are stuck. An elegant word used merely to use an elegant word is bombastic . . . er . . . big sounding and unnatural.

> A college essay is not the place to show off your vocabulary.

Simple ideas dressed up in ornate words often obscure meaning. Worse, they make the writer sound phony, if not foolish. For example, you wouldn't say, "I'm going to my *domicile*" after a day at school, and you don't call your teachers *pedagogues*. Yet, this overblown sentence appeared on the draft of an essay for Northwestern: "My history pedagogue insisted that I labor in my domicile for two hours each night." How much clearer to have written, "My history teacher assigned two hours' homework every night."

Notice how clear these sentences sound when the inflated words are removed:

FANCY

The more I recalled her degradation of me, the more inexorable I became.

PLAIN

The more I thought of her insults, the more determined I grew.

FANCY

During that year, my proclivities toward blogging were instigated.

PLAIN

During that year, I became an avid blogger.

FANCY

I learned the importance of cordiality and cooperation in a competitive racing situation.

PLAIN

I learned that teamwork pays off in a race.

Please don't interpret this plea for plain words as an endorsement of everyday slang. If you need an expression like *pure dead brilliant, phat-phree,* and *KPC,* or a comic-book word like *gonna* and *gotta,* by all means use it. For heaven's sake, though, use such words sparingly and only to create an effect you can't do without. Don't highlight a word with "quotes" to signal that you know it's nonstandard. If, to make its point, your essay overdoses on slang, be sure to show your mastery of standard English by writing another part of your application in good, straightforward prose.

English is loaded with simple words that can express the most profound ideas. Descartes' famous observation, "I think, therefore, I am," reshaped forever the way we think about existence. Descartes may have used esoteric language to make his point, but the very simplicity of his words endows his statement with great power. Ernest Hemingway called a writer's greatest gift "a built-in, shock-proof crap detector." Hemingway's own detector worked well. He produced about the leanest, plainest writing in the English language—not that you should try to emulate Hemingway, although you could do worse, but an efficient crap detector will encourage you to choose words only because they say exactly what you mean.

Exact Words

It's often hard to break the habit of using vague, shadowy, and abstract words. If you want your ideas to sink into the minds of readers, however, give them exact, clear, and well-defined words. Almost always, exact words help you express exact thoughts. Since a tight, precise, hard-edged word has an unmistakable meaning, give the reader a *wooden bucket* instead of a *container,* a *blazing sunset* instead of a *beautiful evening, white-haired and stooped* instead of *old,* and a *Big Mac, large fries, and Coke* instead of *lunch.*

To write with exact words is to write with pictures, sounds, and actions that are as vivid in words as in reality. Exact words hit harder than hazy ones:

HAZY

Quite violently, I expressed my anger to the other team's player.

EXACT

I punched the Bruins' goalie in the nose and sent him sprawling.

HAZY

Skiing is a sport I enjoy, not only for the esthetics, but also for the art and skill involved.

EXACT

I like to ski, not just to see snow-decked pines and brilliant sky, but also to weave gracefully down steep slopes.

Of course, you need abstract words, too. Words such as *beauty, love, existence, nobility,* and *envy* stand for ideas that exist in the mind. The power to think in terms of *situations, concepts, feelings,* and *principles* is unique to humans. An essay full of vague, hard-to-define words and ideas, though, will leave your reader at sea about what you are trying to say. A student who writes about an "ugly" teacher, for example, sends a different image of an ugly person to each reader. If the teacher is *a ragged, slouching shrew,* the writer should say so. Or if the teacher's personality is ugly, the student should write *ill-tempered and aloof* or show the teacher shouting harsh threats at the hapless class.

Anticipate reactions to every word. Ask yourself, "Might readers understand this word in any other way than how I meant it?" If so, strike it out and find another.

Although exact words will always be clearer than abstract ones, a word or phrase with multiple meanings may often help to tighten your writing. Every time you mention *dinner,* for example, you need not list the menu. Be aware, though, that nobody will care to read an essay that forgot to come down to earth.

Clear Sentences

Short sentences are the clearest—sometimes. Use a short sentence to emphasize a point. Sometimes you may need long sentences to convey complex ideas, although a complex thought may just as easily be expressed in clear, short sentences. When trapped in a long, strung-out sentence, break it into a set of shorter sentences. Later, if necessary, you can put the pieces together again.

Now and then you may run into a long-winded sentence that suffers from paralysis. No matter how you tinker with it you can't make it move without damaging its meaning. Walk away from it and repair it later, or try a few manipulations. Here, to illustrate a stubborn case, is a rambling bit of prose that needs fixing:

> A sentence can be molded into almost any shape, beautiful or ugly.

> One of my biggest rewards has been membership in the Science Alliance, which was formed in my junior year, at which time the alliance members were informed by the chairman of the science department, Dr. Rich, that they could serve as mentors to fifth graders at the district's elementary schools to coach them through hands-on scientific experiments using advanced scientific methods and computer technology.

REMEDY

Break the long sentence into shorter ones.

RESULTS (Some Better Than Others)

One of my biggest rewards has been the Science Alliance. It was formed in my junior year. When the Science Alliance started, Dr. Rich, the chairman of the science department, informed students about a new program. The program made arrangements for members to team up with fifth graders at the district's elementary schools. We would coach the fifth graders on how to conduct hands-on scientific experiments. During these experiments the students would be taught to use advanced scientific methods and computer technology.

or

One of my biggest rewards has been the Science Alliance, formed in my junior year. The organization's purpose, according to Dr. Rich, the science department chairman, was to mentor fifth graders at the district's elementary schools. As a mentor for two years, I have coached boys and girls in the fifth grade on how to conduct hands-on scientific experiments using advanced scientific methods and computer technology.

Move words from predicate to subject.

The Science Alliance has been one of my biggest rewards . . .

The Science Alliance, formed in my junior year, has been one of my biggest rewards.

or

Combine ideas; turn less important ideas into phrases.

Formed in my junior year, the Science Alliance . . .

Change nouns to adjectives.

My most rewarding activity has been the Science Alliance.

Change nouns to verbs.

Science Alliance work has rewarded me . . .

Change verbs to nouns.

The formation of the Science Alliance . . .

Switch the focus.

The Science Alliance introduced me to the rewards of working with fifth graders in . . .

My school's science department chairman, Dr. Rich, introduced me to the most rewarding work, . . .

I got my start as a mentor in science after Dr. Rich formed the Science Alliance, . . .

Once you start such sentence manipulations, you may begin to see endless possibilities. A sentence is much like clay. It's malleable and can be molded into almost any shape, beautiful or ugly. In the end the sentence should stand in the form that expresses most clearly and accurately what you want to say.

Clear Meaning

In your writing, words must fit together like the pieces of a jigsaw puzzle. Sometimes a word looks as though it fits, but it doesn't. A misplaced word may produce a rather peculiar sentence. Take these, for example:

> While running to English class, the bell rang.
> Working full-time, the summer went by quickly.
> When only eight years old, my father warned me about smoking.

These may not strike you as funny at first. Look again. Do you see that these sentences describe a weird world in which bells run to class, summers hold full-time jobs, and youthful fathers dispense advice?

The authors of these sentences have tried to join two pieces that don't fit. The grammar is flawless; the spelling and punctuation are perfect. Even the writers' intentions are clear. In each sentence, however, the parts are mismatched. After the comma in each, readers expect to find out who is running, who was working, and who is just eight years old. They don't. They're left dangling. (Hence, the name *dangling modifier* or *dangling participle* has been assigned to this type of sentence construction.)

To keep the reader from dangling, the writers might have said:

> While the boys were running to English class, the bell rang.
> Since Charlotte worked full-time, her summer sped by.
> When I was eight, my father warned me about smoking.

Relative pronouns (*who, whose, whom, that,* and *which*) may also lead to problems of clarity. Perhaps such words may not deserve a reputation as troublemakers, but like a black sheep in the family, they have it just the same. They've acquired their name—*relative* pronoun—from their intimate relationship with another word in the same sentence, called an *antecedent.*

A relative pronoun and an antecedent are related because one refers directly to the other. In this sentence,

> It's always my brother who is blamed for trouble in the neighborhood.

the relative pronoun "*who*" and the antecedent "*brother*" are right next to each other, about as close as kin can be. In this sentence,

> It's always my brother, now approaching his twentieth birthday, who is blamed for trouble in the neighborhood.

the phrase "*now approaching his twentieth birthday*" intrudes, thereby weakening the relationship, but the meaning is still clear.

You run into a particular problem with pronouns when you try to establish a tie between the pronoun *which*, for example, and a whole series of actions, feelings, or words, as in

> First we had lunch and then our guide told us the secret of the cave, which pleased me.

A reader might honestly wonder what was "pleasing." The cave's secret? The guide's spilling the beans? Lunch? That the secret was revealed after lunch? The pronoun *"which"* might refer to all or to only one of these possible antecedents. It's just not clear. To repair the sentence you might change it into something like this:

> I was pleased that the guide waited until after lunch to tell us the secret of the cave.

If another meaning was intended,

> I was pleased with the secret of the cave, which the guide told us after lunch.

Another sort of pronoun, namely the word *this,* creates similar problems of clarity. Any time you start a sentence with *this,* double-check it. Make sure it refers directly to what you want it to refer. This is advice you should not ignore!

Harmony

Writers, like dancers, strive for harmony in their art. Every hoofer, hip-hopper, belly dancer, and ballerina works hard to achieve grace and balance, and you can tell in an instant whether they've succeeded. So it is when you write an essay. All the parts must fit together. An awkward, incoherent essay—one in which the pieces seem unconnected—will leave your readers disappointed.

As you edit your application essay, therefore, read it over again and again—not until it drives you nuts, but almost. Check it meticulously to see if one idea leads naturally and easily to the next. Look for words and phrases that tie ideas together. (Turn to page 105 for some common examples of transitions.) In a harmonious essay, virtually every sentence bears some sort of reference to the sentence that came before. Such references might be obvious, as in "furthermore" or "for example." Connections are often more subtle than that, however, as in this pair of sentences:

> I have an idealized image in my mind of families that are close, loving, laughing, generous, and supportive.
> I wish that I could find *such qualities* in mine.

Notice that the italicized phrase in the second sentence refers directly to adjectives listed in the first.

Sometimes allusions to previous sentences are carried in the meaning rather than by a specific word or phrase:

> I had a hard time finding his house in the dark.
> I *picked out what I thought should be the address* and knocked at the front door.

In this example the italicized words establish a link to the idea stated in the first sentence. In the second sentence the speaker feels unsure of an address. You know the reason (because it's dark outside) only because you know what the first sentence says.

Search your essay for transitions of all kinds. Whenever you discover a series of three or more sentences devoid of transitions, you may be stuck with a hard-to-read muddle on your hands. Before you do any heavy rewriting, though, try inserting appropriate transitional words, phrases, and sentences. Don't wedge one in where it doesn't belong, however. This could confuse your readers even more.

As you've no doubt realized, editing a piece of writing is a painstaking process. When you examine every word you write, it's easy to drown in a sea of minutiae. Therefore, it helps now and then to stop fussing over the details and to inspect your essay as a whole. Say aloud to yourself or to anyone within earshot, "The point of my essay is . . ." Complete the statement with one clear, straightforward declarative sentence. If it takes more than a single statement, perhaps your essay isn't sufficiently focused. You may be trying to say more than you have space for.

> Now and then, stop fussing over details, and inspect your essay as a whole.

After you've declared your main point, try to say what each part adds to the whole. If any part doesn't contribute, cast it away. You don't need material that sends readers off the course you've set for them. By attending to the contents of the whole essay, you are in a sense checking its harmony, determining whether all its parts work together.

An outline of your essay will help, too. Such an outline need not follow the formal pattern you may have learned in school, but the same principles apply. That is, all the minor pieces, when added together, should equal the whole. In the language of writers, every sentence in a paragraph supports the main idea of the paragraph, and every paragraph supports the main idea of the essay. You'll know that you have a well-structured, harmonious piece of writing when you can't reasonably remove a piece without causing damage to the whole.

Editing for Interest

Don't bore your readers. Admissions officials may ignore an occasional lapse in clarity and even overlook a flaw in grammar, but if your essay bores them, they'll lose interest in both you and your essay.

Like most applicants, you've probably led a fairly routine life. That's no reason, however, to write a routine essay. Fortunately, there are plenty of techniques for turning an ordinary piece of writing into a highly readable and stylish essay.

Brevity Works Best

Never use two words when one will do. Readers want to be told quickly and directly what you have to say. Wordiness sucks the life out of your writing. Cut out needless words. Readers value economy.

(Stop! Go back to the previous paragraph. Do you see the unnecessary words? Did you notice that the next-to-last sentence reiterates the first? Yes, the statement contains only four words, but are those words necessary? Do they merely add weight—and no substance—to the paragraph?)

Your sentences, like muscles, should be firm and tight. Needless words are flabby. Trim the fat. Make your writing lean. As you edit, exercise your crossing-out muscles.

Go through every sentence and cross out extra words. The sentence you just read contains nine words (forty-three letters). It could be trimmed still more. For example, "Cut extra words out of every sentence" (seven words, thirty-one letters). When the sentence was first written, it read, "The writer should work through all the sentences he writes by examining each one and crossing out all the extra words" (twenty-one words, ninety-seven letters)—

three times longer than the trim, seven-word model, and many times duller.

In lean writing every word counts. One missing word distorts or changes the meaning. To trim your sentences, squeeze them through your fat detector:

1. Look for repetition. Then combine sentences.

FAT

In tenth grade I accepted a position at Wilkins' Fabrics. In this position I learned about fabrics and about how to handle customers. (23 words)

TRIMMED

In tenth grade I accepted a position at Wilkins' Fabrics, where I learned about fabrics and handling customers. (18)

RETRIMMED

Working at Wilkins' Fabrics since tenth grade, I have learned to handle both fabrics and customers. (16)

2. Look for telltale words like *which, who, that, thing,* and *all.* They may indicate the presence of fat.

FAT

Manicotti is a dish *that* I always enjoy eating. (9)

TRIMMED

I like manicotti any time. (5)

FAT

Jogging has been a wonderful activity, *which* has stimulated my body and freed my mind to think. (17)

TRIMMED

Jogging has been wonderful for stimulating my body and freeing my mind. (12)

FAT

The *thing* that made me angry was mosquitoes inside my shirt. (11)

TRIMMED

Mosquitoes inside my shirt angered me. (6)

3. Look for phrases that add words but little meaning.

FAT

At this point in time, I am not able to say. (11)

TRIMMED

I can't say now. (4)

FAT

The chef stayed home *as a result of* his not feeling well. (12)

TRIMMED

The chef stayed home because he felt sick. (8)

A Baker's Dozen Specially Selected Fat Phrases—No, Make That Thirteen Selected Fat Phrases:

FAT	*TRIMMED*
what I mean is	I mean
after all is said and done	finally
for all intents and purposes	(omit)
in the final analysis	finally
few and far between	few
each and every one	each
this is a subject that	this subject
ten in number	ten
at the age of six years old	at age six
most unique	unique
true fact	fact
biography of his life	biography
in regard to, with regard to, in relation to, with reference to	about

Readers are too busy for sentences stuffed with fat phrases.

After your sentences are pared to the bone, look at what remains and get ready to cut some more. Although it hurts to take out what you worked hard to put in, the writing will be stronger, more readable, and noticeably more interesting.

Show, Don't Tell

The genius who invented "show and tell" realized that seeing a pet frog or a souvenir model of Grant's Tomb was far more interesting to an audience than just hearing about it. Since writers can't use hands, make faces, or dangle an object in front of readers, they must rely on words to do both the telling and the showing.

> Show more than you tell. Use words to make the reader see.

Show more than you tell. Use words to make the reader *see*. For example, don't leave the reader guessing about Laura's beautiful hair. *Show* how the breeze catches the edge of her silky, brown hair. Don't just tell about the garbage in the hallway. *Show* the splintered glass lying in the oily water, the half-torn notebook, and the newspaper, yellowed with age. Don't just say you felt happy. *Show* yourself bounding down the steps four at a time, coat unzipped, shouting into the wind, "Hurray, I did it!"

TELL

After I won, I experienced a wonderful and unique feeling, which makes me want to win again.

SHOW

After I won, my sense of accomplishment grew with every handshake and pat on the back. My face ached from grinning so much. I knew that I'd be back next year to win again.

TELL

There is so much I have to do after school that I often don't even have time for homework.

SHOW

The busy part of my life starts at three o'clock: pick up Scott, my baby brother; piano lessons on Tuesdays at four; French Club; work on the newspaper; and tutor my neighbor in math. I don't have time for homework, not to mention working out.

When words show what you have in mind, the reader can see and feel and hear what you saw and felt and heard. It takes details—lots and lots of them—to make a sight or sound or smell as real for the reader as it is for you.

Your essay would soon grow tedious—both to write and to read—if you showed every grain of sand on the beach. Be selective. Show readers the sights you want them to *see:* the gleaming sand and fragments of clam shells; to *hear:* the squawk of gulls and children's shouts; to *smell:* salt spray, seaweed, and suntan oil; to *feel:* stinging feet and sweaty, sun-baked backs; and to *taste:* gritty egg salad sandwiches and parched, salt-caked lips.

Although too much detail can be boring, too little is just as bad. A balance is best. No one can tell you exactly how to achieve that balance. You need time to get the feel of it. Like walking a tightrope, riding a bike, or doing a back flip, it becomes instinct after a while. The context, as well as your judgment of the reader's intelligence, will have to determine how detailed you need to be. To get the knack a little more quickly, study a written passage that you found interesting. Pick out both details and broad statements. Use the passage as a general model for your own writing, but give it your own stamp. After all, it's your voice the reader wants to hear.

Active Verbs

At some point you must have learned that a verb is a word that shows *action* or *state of being*. That's a fair description of a verb if you're learning grammar. To an essay writer, however, knowing that *action* verbs differ from *being* verbs is far more important. You need active verbs to stimulate interest. Since active verbs

> Active verbs pump life into your writing.

describe or show movement, they create life. They perform, stir up, get up, and move around. They excel over all other words in their power to pump vitality into your writing. They add energy and variety to sentences. As a bonus, active verbs often help you trim needless words from your writing.

In contrast, *being* verbs are stagnant. They don't do anything. Notice the lifelessness in all the most common forms of the verb *to be: is, are, was, were, am, has been, had been, will be.* When used in a sentence, each of these being verbs joins the subject to the predicate—and that's all. In fact, the verb *to be* acts much like an equals sign in an equation, as in "Four minus three is one" ($4 - 3 = 1$), "Harold is smart" (Harold = smart), or "That is some spicy meatball" (That = SSMB). Because equals signs (and being verbs) show no action, use active verbs whenever you can.

Being verbs are perfectly acceptable in speech and writing. In fact, it's hard to get along without them. Be stingy, however. If more than, say, one-fourth of your sentences use a form of *to be* as the main verb, perhaps you're relying too heavily on being verbs.

Substitute active verbs for being verbs by extracting them from other words in the same sentence. For instance:

BEING VERB

Linda was the winner of the raffle.

ACTIVE VERB

Linda won the raffle.
Here the verb *"won"* has been extracted from the noun *"winner."*
Active verbs may also be extracted from adjectives, as in:

BEING VERB

My summer at the New Jersey shore was enjoyable.

ACTIVE VERB

I enjoyed my summer at the New Jersey shore.
Sometimes it pays to substitute an altogether fresh verb.

BEING VERB

It is not easy for me to express my feelings.

ACTIVE VERB

I find it difficult to express my feelings.

BEING VERB

There was a distant wailing of an ambulance.

ACTIVE VERB

We heard the distant wailing of an ambulance.

Practice will help you purge being verbs from your sentences and add vitality to whatever you write.

The noun you employ as the subject of a sentence will often determine your chances of using a lively verb. Abstract nouns limit your opportunities. For example, you're almost compelled to use a form of *to be* in any sentence that begins with *"The reason,"* as in *"The reason I am applying to Colgate* is. . . ." You have few verb choices, too, when the subject of the sentence is *thought, concept, idea, issue, way, cause,* or any other abstract noun.

On the other hand, nouns that stand for specific people, places, events, and objects take active verbs easily. When your sentence contains a subject that can do something—a person, for instance— you can choose from among thousands of active verbs. Anytime you replace a general or abstract noun with a solid, easy-to-define noun, you are likely to end up with a tight, energetic, and generally more interesting sentence:

ABSTRACT SUBJECT

The issue was settled by Mrs. Marino.

DEFINITE SUBJECT

Mrs. Marino settled the issue.

ABSTRACT SUBJECT

The cause of the strike was the students' demand for peace.

DEFINITE SUBJECT

The students struck for peace.

ABSTRACT SUBJECT

The way to Memorial Hospital is down this road.

DEFINITE SUBJECT

This road goes to Memorial Hospital.

Being verbs aren't alone in their dullness. They share that distinction with *have, come, go, make, move,* and *get.* These common verbs do little to enliven writing. Each has so many different uses that they creep into sentences virtually unnoticed. Use them freely in contexts where they fit, of course, but stay alert for more vivid and lively substitutes.

Active Sentences

Most events in life don't just occur by themselves. Somebody does something, somebody *acts*. Hamburgers don't just get eaten. People—Julie, Paul, and Mr. Dolan— eat them. Marriages don't just happen; men and women deliberately go out and marry each other. Touchdowns don't score, jails don't just fill up, graves aren't dug, cotton isn't picked, and herring do not simply get caught and stuffed into jars. People do all these things.

> To create interest, take advantage of your readers' natural curiosity about others.

The deeds that people do register quickly on a reader's mind. To create interest in your writing, therefore, take advantage of your reader's natural curiosity about others. Always write active sentences. Even those sentences in which no specific action occurs can be written in an "active," rather than a "passive," voice.

For example, consider who performed an action in this sentence:

> Six nights a week were spent in preparation for the concert by our class.

Clearly, the class acted. More precisely, it rehearsed for a concert, but the sentence keeps you waiting until the end to tell you who performed an action. Moreover, by placing "our class" at the end, the writer has been obliged to use the passive verb, "*were spent.*" If you relocate "our class" to the beginning of the sentence, you suddenly activate the whole statement:

> Our class rehearsed six nights a week in preparation for the concert.

The change not only tightens and enlivens the sentence, it adds interest. You derive the same results any time you turn passive sentences into active ones:

PASSIVE

Every day, the newspaper was brought home by my father.

ACTIVE

My father brought home the newspaper every day.

PASSIVE

Rutgers was attended by my brother, my cousin, and three of my uncles.

ACTIVE

My brother, my cousin, and three uncles went to Rutgers.

Although active sentences are usually more natural, compact, and interesting, to avoid awkwardness you may occasionally need to use the passive voice when you are uncertain who performed an action, for instance, or when it isn't important to say:

PASSIVE

The blue curtain was raised at 8:30.

ACTIVE

At 8:30, a stagehand (or Mary Ann, a production assistant) raised the curtain.

In the passive sentence curtain time is the important fact. Who pulled the rope is immaterial.

Fresh Language and Surprises

Fresh language (1) stimulates the mind, (2) pleases the ear, and (3) surprises the emotions—all praiseworthy effects of a college essay. Dull writing, on the other hand, is predictable. That is, you can almost tell what word is likely to come next in a sentence. When readers know what to expect, they'll soon lose interest, both in the writing and its author. If you serve up verbal surprises, however, your readers will stick with you.

You don't need rare or unusual words to surprise your readers. A common word, deftly used, will do:

ORDINARY

I was ten before I saw my first pigeon.

SURPRISING

I was ten before I met my first pigeon.

Since people don't normally *meet* pigeons, the unexpected shift from *saw* to *met* creates a small surprise.

ORDINARY

The shark bit the swimmers.

SURPRISING

The shark dined on the swimmers.

Changing the verb *bit* to *dined* makes a common sentence uncommon, because the word *dined* suggests good manners and gentility, pleasures that few sharks enjoy.

Sounds can create surprises, too. Some words match the sounds they describe. The word *bombard,* for example, makes a heavy, explosive sound. *Yawn* has a wide-open sound that can be stretched out indefinitely. *Choke* sticks in your throat. *Murmuring streams* evokes the sound of—what else?

> When you surprise your readers, they'll stick with you.

A reader often derives unexpected pleasure from the repetition of sounds—either consonants or vowels—as in *"The dark, dank day smelled of death"* or *"The machine sucked up the sewage in the swamp."* You probably shouldn't repeat sounds too often because they may distract the reader from the meaning of your words, but an occasional treat for the ear builds interest in your writing.

Surprise with Comparisons

It isn't easy to find just the right word to express all you think, sense, and do. How, for instance, do you show the look a toll collector gave you, or how do you describe six-in-the-morning street sounds? What about the taste of stale Coke, the smell of rotting garbage, the feel of clean sheets, a fear, a frustration?

> With comparisons you can express the inexpressible.

Writers often catch those elusive details and fleeting sensations by making comparisons. An original comparison will not only delight your reader but will provide you with words to express your most inexpressible ideas. In addition, comparisons are economical. They require fewer words than you might otherwise need to state an idea.

To describe old men in a nursing home, for instance, you could show their creased faces, the folds of papery skin at their throats, the pale, cracked lips, and the white stubble on their chins. If you don't need all those details in your essay, you could simply compare the men to slats on weathered wooden fences. Instantly your reader will get the picture. Yes, the rough gray texture of weather-beaten boards does suggest withered men lined up in a nursing home corridor, a likeness that probably hadn't occurred to the reader before.

Small children usually don't know enough words to express all they want to say. By nature, therefore, they make comparisons: "Daddy, when my foot goes to sleep, it feels like ginger ale." As people get older, they often lose the knack and have to relearn it. When you consciously seek comparisons, though, you'll find them sprouting everywhere—like weeds. Compare, for example, the taste of fruit punch to antifreeze, a sweet look to something you'd pour on waffles, a friend's voice to a chicken's cackle, the smell of a locker room to rotting hay.

Figures of speech, such as similes (Tom wrestles *like* a tiger) and metaphors (Tom *is* a tiger), are types of comparisons. They help the writer point out likenesses between something familiar (tiger) and something unfamiliar (Tom the wrestler). One side of the comparison must always be common and recognizable. Therefore, comparing the cry of the Arctic tern to the song of a tree toad won't help a reader familiar with neither water birds nor tree toads. Since most people know what a fiddle sounds like, a more revealing comparison would be: *The cry of the Arctic tern sounds like a fiddler tuning up.*

American English is littered with hundreds of metaphors and similes, once fresh and surprising, but now dried out and lifeless. Avoid these like the plague. *"Like the plague,"* in fact, is one you should avoid. Figures of speech like *"high as a kite"* and *"pale as a ghost"* have lost their zing. Don't resurrect them in your essay. Let them rest in the cliché graveyard.

At one time, every familiar combination of words, such as *"you've got to be kidding"* and *"I couldn't care less"* was new, witty, or poetic. Such expressions were so striking that people, thinking that they would seem up to date, witty, or poetic, used them over and over. Constant use dulled them and turned them into clichés. No reader will delight in a cliché. By definition, a cliché has lost its kick.

A TREASURY OF WORN-OUT PHRASES AND EXPRESSIONS TO BE AVOIDED

bummed out	to think out of the box
how does that sit with you?	would you believe?
to touch base with	go off the deep end
off the top of my head	shag some rays
try an idea on for size	for openers
how does that grab you?	flipped out
the bottom line is . . .	get off my back
having said that . . .	off the wall
throw out the baby with the bath water	no way, José
I'm getting psyched	many things on my plate
for all intents and purposes	

There are countless others to guard against. The number is *awesome*. They sneak into writing *when your back is turned,* when *your defenses are down,* and *when you least expect them.* Beware!

To avoid overused expressions, ask yourself whether you've ever heard or seen the phrase before. If you have, drop it, not *like a hot potato,* but just as quickly.

Sentence Variety

Sentence variety keeps readers awake, alert, and interested.

Monotony kills interest. A steady diet of mashed potatoes dulls the taste buds. A 200-mile stretch on a straight road takes the joy out of driving. Day after day of routine rots the brain. Listening too often to the same song destroys its charm. So it is with writing an essay. Repetition of the same sentence pattern makes readers wish they didn't have to read any further. Keep your readers awake, alert, and interested by serving up a variety of sentence patterns.

Most English sentences begin with the subject, as in

> My sister got married last summer in a hot-air balloon 1,000 feet over Connecticut.

To avoid the monotony of many successive sentences in the same pattern, move the subject elsewhere and look for other ways to start a sentence:

> In a hot-air balloon 1,000 feet over Connecticut, my sister married her high school sweetheart, Jack.

After an initial prepositional phrase, the writer named the subject, "*my sister.*"

> Surprisingly, ten people witnessed the wedding—five in the same balloon basket, and five in another.

Obviously, the writer began this sentence with an adverb.

> When word got out about the wedding site, reporters hounded the couple for days.

After introducing this sentence with a dependent clause, the writer named the subject, "*reporters,*" and then added the rest of the sentence.

> Still, the ceremony itself was held without fanfare.

This writer snuck in the subject after an opening connective.

> To keep the wedding quiet, Jack and Annie kept the date to themselves until the night before the flight.

To compose the sentence, the writer began with a *verbal,* in this instance the infinitive form of the verb *keep.* Verbals look and feel like verbs, but aren't. At least they're not the verbs that groups of words need to qualify as complete sentences. Verbals come from verbs, though, which explains the resemblance.

> Drinking champagne, the guests flew for an hour before landing on a par-four fairway of a golf course.

Hoping to keep the reader's interest, this writer began the sentence with another kind of verbal—a participle. Very often the *i-n-g* ending indicates that you've used a participle.

> Thrilled by the adventure, the wedding party vowed to fly again on Jack and Annie's first anniversary.

Determined to begin a sentence with another kind of verbal, the writer chose a verb with an *ed* ending, which functions like an adjective.

Still another appealing variation is the sentence containing a paired construction. In such a sentence, you have two equal and matched ideas. Sometimes the ideas differ only by one or two words, as in: *"It wasn't that I was turning away from my family, it was my family that was turning away from me"* or *"While I put my heart into dancing, dancing worked its way into my heart."* The strength of such sentences lies in the balance of parallel parts. Each part could stand alone, but together the idea has more muscle.

Once in a great while, you can create interest by reversing the usual order of words in a sentence. If used too often, the writing will sound stilted and unnatural, but look at the power you get out of a sentence that begins with an adjective that you want the reader to remember: *"Desperate I grew when the telegram hadn't arrived."* Likewise, an inverted statement—*"A math genius I am not"*—carries a lot more punch than *"I am not a math genius."* Use inverted sentences cautiously, though. In the wrong place they'll sound silly.

Lucky is the writer in search of variety, for English contains a huge selection of sentence types, many of which you probably learned about in school. Obviously, there are long and short sentences. At your fingertips you also have simple, compound, and complex sentences. You have declarative, interrogative, imperative, and exclamatory sentences. You can write sentences interrupted in midstream by a dash—although some people will tell you it's not quite proper. You can also use direct and indirect quotes, and once in a great while—to drive home a point—a single emphatic word. Perfect!

With so many choices, there's no excuse for writing humdrum sentences that march monotonously through your essay. Please your reader with combinations and variations. Don't mix up sentence types just to mix up sentence types, however. You may end up with a mess on your hands. Always be guided by what seems clearest and by what seems varied enough to hold your reader's interest.

A Note on Repetition

On occasion, skillful use of repetition enables you to stress an idea in an unusual way. At first glance, for example, this passage from Sally McC's essay appears repetitive:

> My grandmother raised me. She took pride in her five grandchildren. She introduced me to theater and ballet. She sat patiently through my piano and dance recitals. She sent me to sleep-away camp every summer. She did all a mother is expected to do except live long enough to see me applying to Smith, her alma mater.

Every sentence but the first starts with the same word. Yet, the paragraph isn't monotonous. What strikes you is not the similarity of the sentences, but the grandmother's devotion to child rearing. In this instance, Sally used repetition to her advantage.

Short and Long Sentences

Sentences come in all lengths, from one word to thousands. A long sentence demands greater effort from readers because, while stepping from one part of the sentence to the next, they must keep track of more words, modifiers, phrases (not to speak of parenthetical asides), and clauses without losing the writer's main thought, which may be buried amid any number of secondary, or less important, thoughts. Short sentences are easier to grasp. A brief sentence makes its point quickly and sometimes with considerable potency, as in this passage from Tracy P's essay about a trip to Florida:

> A balance of short and long sentences works best.

> For a day and a night the five of us—my parents, two sisters and I—sat upright in our van and drove and drove and drove. For thirty hours we shared our thoughts and dreams, counted McDonald's, told stories, ate granola bars, drank juice, dozed, played games on our laptops, sat wordlessly, and finally, by the water in Daytona, we watched a brilliant crimson sun rise out of the Atlantic. But mostly, we argued.

The brief sentence at the end jolts the reader. Its bluntness, especially after a windy, forty-four-word sentence, produces a mild shock. Placing a tight, terse sentence next to a lengthy one creates a startling effect. The technique, however, works best when used only rarely. Overuse dilutes its impact.

Also, several short sentences in a row can be as tiresome as a string of long, complex sentences. A balance works best. If you have strung together four or five equally long (or short) sentences, separate (or combine) them. Here, to illustrate, is a drawn-out sentence in need of dismemberment:

> Because I was certain that it would be all right, without waiting for the approval of my mother, who was not yet home from the hospital after her operation for a back ailment that had been troubling her for years—in fact, ever since her automobile accident on the way to Chicago one Christmas, I decided during spring vacation to apply for a job as a counselor at a summer camp for children, six to fourteen years old, in Brookdale, a tiny village close to my uncle's farm in Wisconsin.

To lighten the load of an extended sentence like this, you could divide it, rearrange it, add verbs, drop an idea or two, change the emphasis, and cut words. You could employ some of the sentence-fixing tools described on pages 136 to 139. When you're done, the ideas, now clearer and more streamlined, might sound something like this:

> During spring vacation I applied for a counselor's job at a summer camp in the tiny village of Brookdale, Wisconsin. The camp, for six- to fourteen-year-olds, is near my uncle's farm. I was certain my mother wouldn't mind. So I didn't wait for her to return from the hospital, where she was recuperating from an operation for a back ailment.

Conversely, you achieve greater balance when you combine a string of several very short sentences. For instance:

> I live in two environments. I was born in Canada. I lived there for ten years. Then we moved to Boston. That was an important event. It was painful. The kids in Boston were cold and distant. All my friends were in Montreal.

Although the terse sentences may vaguely suggest the writer's despair, the writing style calls to mind a grade school primer. Greater fluidity and grace are expected from college applicants. The passage cries out for revision—perhaps something like this:

> I am from two environments, one Canadian and one American. I was born in Montreal, but moved to Boston at age ten. The move was painful. Cold and distant acquaintances surrounded me in Boston. Friends lived in Montreal.

Note that you frequently get a small bonus when you combine sentences: Your writing gets more active and less wordy—both worthy goals for a writer.

The Final Check

If you took the task of editing seriously, your essay should now be in very good shape, maybe in better shape than you are. Many writers, even the best, sometimes don't know whether their hard labor and sacrifice are worth it. They can't tell whether they've done a good job. Self-doubt is the writer's trademark, the price you pay for a clear, precise, interesting, and correct essay.

Although your essay may half-sicken you by now, stick with it just a little longer. It's probably better than you think. After all, you're not a professional writer so you shouldn't expect to write like one. High school quarterbacks don't play for the Dallas Cowboys, high school actors don't win Emmys, and high school writers—even the best of them—can't compete with the pros. Chances are you've written a decent essay that will stand up in any college admissions office. Your struggle to get the words right has probably paid off. You've revised and edited, re-revised and re-edited. Good! You added, cut, switched parts around. Very good! That shows you've been thinking. You logged plenty of computer time. You walked away, came back, tried again. Perhaps you wrote ten times as many words as you actually used.

Finally, you got the words the way you wanted them—the way they should be. You survived the ordeal, and the reader in the admissions office, who doesn't know you yet—but soon will—will be happy to make your acquaintance.

Before you send in the final version of your essay, check the whole thing one more time. Don't be satisfied until you can answer YES! to all the questions on this Editing Checklist:

	YES!	MOSTLY	HARDLY	NO
Does the essay *sound* like you?	❑	❑	❑	❑
Have you used *plain* words?	❑	❑	❑	❑
Have you used *exact* language?	❑	❑	❑	❑
Does your essay have *focus*?	❑	❑	❑	❑
Are all parts in *harmony*?	❑	❑	❑	❑
Is each sentence *accurately* worded?	❑	❑	❑	❑
Have you *trimmed* needless words?	❑	❑	❑	❑
Do you *show* more than *tell*?	❑	❑	❑	❑
Have you used *active verbs*?	❑	❑	❑	❑
Is your language *fresh*?	❑	❑	❑	❑
Do you include verbal *surprises*?	❑	❑	❑	❑
Are your sentences *varied*?	❑	❑	❑	❑
Is sentence length *balanced*?	❑	❑	❑	❑

6 PRESENTING YOUR ESSAY

Would you like to hear a sad but true story? It's about Scott, a high school senior, a good student—even a brilliant one—with a keen desire to go to Oberlin. Following the application instructions on the Oberlin website, he submitted the college's supplement to the Common Application weeks before he planned to complete the standard Commonapp. He wrote the essay for the supplement in less than an hour. He didn't give it a second reading, didn't proof it, didn't run the text through his computer's spell-checker. Frankly, he didn't even answer the question that was asked.

Oberlin's admission people concluded that Scott couldn't be serious about attending Oberlin if he submitted what they called a "third-rate" effort. In a word, they told him, "Forget it!" and advised him not to bother with the remainder of the application.

Obviously, there's a lesson in Scott's tale: Present your essay with pride, as close to perfect as you can make it.

Online and Paper Applications

Most colleges prefer that you apply online. Many insist on it, and some waive the application fee if you do. An essay prepared online should be presented in 12-point or 10-point type—nothing smaller. Use an ordinary font like Times or Garamond, similar to the print in this book. Avoid exotic fonts like Vivaldi and Pristina. They may look pretty but cannot be read easily.

> Most colleges prefer that your write your essay online.

Double-spaced or 1.5-spaced text is preferable to single-space. Katie Fretwell, the Amherst College director of admission, observes "Admission committees are not likely to award 'extra credit' for fancy fonts or perfect calligraphy." University of Vermont's admission associate Susan Wertheimer urges students to prepare distraction-free essays. "Fancy graphics, tiny fonts to compress lots of text onto one page, or large fonts to use up space are often mere annoyances," she says. "You *do* want your essay to stand out but not for the wrong reasons."

If you use a paper application, either mailed to you from the college or one you've downloaded from the college's Website as a PDF file, use high-quality white paper, 8½ by 11 inches. If the application leaves space for written responses, it is perfectly fine to print your words on a computer, then neatly trim the sheet and attach it to the application. But adhere to the instructions. Guidelines such as "Use only the space provided" should be taken seriously. So should word limits. Colleges mean business when they say write 250 words. (MIT says "Yes, we'll count.") For most other colleges, though, its permissible to go over or under by, say, ten percent. Too many words (or too few) will count against you. If no limits or guidelines are given, consider the following: Admissions officials must read scores of essays every day. They don't have time to read lengthy, rambling essays. They want a quick take on who you are and what you value. Give it to them as succinctly as possible. An excellent rule of thumb is that two double-spaced pages is the absolute maximum. One and a half pages is even better.

> Don't write more than two double-spaced pages.

To make the presentation of your essay clear and legible, place your text in the middle of the page, leaving at least a one-inch margin all around. Number your pages, and if you are asked to write more than one essay, designate which is which by using the question number or topic from the application.

It goes without saying that cross-outs and last-minute insertions using arrows, asterisks, paragraph markers, or carets are not acceptable. Don't change anything on your final copy unless you are prepared to reprint it. Aim to make your essay letter-perfect. In all respects, neatness counts. Heed the words of Margaret Drugovich, Vice President of Admission at Ohio Wesleyan University: "Hard-to-read essays can be very annoying," she says, "and probably affect the reader's perception of the overall quality of a student's application."

Proofreading

To proofread well, you need fresh eyes. Therefore, your best proofreading method is to let someone else do it. Print five copies of your essay, and have five reliable readers scour your piece for flaws in grammar, punctuation, and spelling.

If you're on your own, put your essay aside for a few days. Then read your essay slowly, once for the sense of it and once for mechanics. Read it a line at a time, keeping a hawklike watch on every letter, word, and mark of punctuation. You might even cut a narrow horizontal window out of a spare sheet of paper. Move the window over your essay a line at a time, concentrating on that line only. Search for missing words, extra words, and flawed grammar and punctuation.

> Read your essay slowly, once for the sense of it and once for the mechanics.

Use the grammar and spell checker on your computer, but remember that the computer won't detect misused words or words that sound alike but take different spellings: *there, their,* and *they're; its* and *it's; to, two,* and *too.* Also, such words as *principal* and *principle, stationary* and *stationery, whether* and *weather,* and dozens of others that trap unwary writers. Students using the Common Application face another potential pitfall, according to the dean of admissions at Denison University, Perry Robinson: "They send the same essay to more than one college and forget to change the name of the college in their essays." Imagine the reaction of a reader in the Denison admissions office discovering that the applicant had "always wanted to go to Colgate."

Getting Help

Show drafts of your essays to people you trust—good friends, a parent, teacher, advisor, or college counselor. When you're facing a tough new assignment like writing a college essay, it's natural to seek a word of encouragement or help. Indeed, you're lucky to know people who will help. If you're willing to pay for help, go to the Internet. Dozens of sites offer

> It's immoral and dangerous to submit an essay that cannot honestly be called yours.

editorial assistance for fees ranging from fifty to several hundred dollars, depending on the number and length of the essays and the type of service you ask for. Getting help from others, though, raises the impossible ethical question: When does your work cease to be yours and become theirs? There's a thin boundary between help and meddling. With luck, your well-meaning helpers won't overstep it.

If you've received suggestions for rewording a sentence or two, changing a few words, or clarifying an idea, you are probably still master of your own essay. If the help consisted of extensive rewriting, bloodying your paper with a river of red ink, and putting words in your mouth, you're about to submit an essay that cannot honestly be called yours. This is not only immoral, it's dangerous.

Books like this one feature essays that worked. Let them inspire you. Sample essays are often published by newspapers and magazines. By all means, read them, and let them trigger ideas for you to write about. Online Websites offer essays for sale or for the taking. With so many model essays at their fingertips, some students can't resist the temptation to lift all or part of an essay they didn't write, submit it, and hope for the best. Jonathan Reider, Senior Associate Director of Admission at Stanford, says, "You'd be surprised by how many copied essays we see. We once had two essays on dance that were clearly copied from the same source. To this day, we don't know what the source was, but we knew the essays were too similar to have been written by accident. We never would have noticed if we had received only one, but since we got two, both applicants were doomed."

People who read college essays for a living know the distinctive style of high school writing. Even the best of it differs from the writing of adults. Perhaps it's the rhythm, the use of a certain word, an unusual turn of phrase, the juxtaposition of ideas—each can tip off a reader that an adult has had a hand in the essay. There are certain usages that, although natural for an experienced adult writer, rarely find their way into a high school student's essay. (The sentence you just read contains just such an example. Notice that the subordinate clause, "although natural for an experienced adult writer," is embedded in the main clause. One in a thousand high school writers is likely to construct a sentence like that. It would be equally rare, too, for a high school student to say "usages . . . find their way." Teenagers usually don't express themselves that way.)

> Get help, but not too much of it.

That's not to say that every ably written application essay will arouse suspicion in the admissions office. Many applicants write superior essays all by themselves. If a student with average English grades and unexceptional College Board scores submits a slick, highly sophisticated essay, however, a reader will notice. When admissions officers have reason to question the authorship of an essay, they'll scrutinize the applicant's school record and search through teachers' recommendations for mention of the student's writing ability. If they still have doubts, they may phone the high school for verification.

Getting substantial help with an essay may reduce your anxiety, but it also does you a disservice. You should make it into the college of your choice based on what you know, what you can do, and who you are. Misrepresenting yourself may get you in, but once on campus *you* will do the work, *you* will do the writing, *you* will sink or swim on your own. An essay that fools the admissions office will grant you a short-lived victory. In a few months, the real you will start bringing home real grades. Your application essay will be history, as will, perhaps, your career as a student at that college.

In Addition to Your Essay

Some colleges want more than an essay from you. They ask for paragraph-long responses to any number of questions—why you chose that particular college, which extracurricular activity you like the most, your favorite book, career plans, honors, and so on. Whatever your answers, write them with the same care as your essay. Start with drafts. Revise and edit. Use your most interesting writing style. Since you're usually limited to less than half a dozen lines, get to the point promptly and express yourself concisely. Be attentive to the sound and style of your responses.

Some questions invite you to reply with a list of some kind—travels, prizes, alumni connections. If you can, respond with a thoughtful, well-developed paragraph. Not only will your answer be more interesting to read, you'll have the opportunity to emphasize the items that matter. Moreover, the reader will note that you took the trouble to write a coherent, lucid paragraph and that your writing repertoire contains more than just a college essay.

When an application asks, "Is there additional information we should know?" try to reply with an emphatic "Yes!" Since your essay won't have told them everything, grab this chance to explain more of yourself or to show your interests and accomplishments. Applicants frequently send their creative work—perhaps a short story, a collection of poetry, articles written for the school paper, slides of artwork, photographs—almost anything that fits into an envelope or small package. Don't overdo it, though. One carefully chosen term paper will suffice to reveal your love of history. One chapter of your novel is more than admissions people will have time to read, anyway. Quality, not quantity, counts.

Whatever you send, prepare it with the same high standards you used on your essay. Written material should be clearly printed; photographs and artwork should be attractively displayed and explained with captions. Before you mail a CD of your music or a DVD of your gymnastic performance, make sure that it contains only what you want the college to hear or see. Also, submit only a few minutes' worth of material—not your whole concert or routine.

Don't feel obliged to create a piece of work just for your college application. Most people don't. It's not their style. Furthermore, most admissions officials realize that high school seniors have enough to do without the burden of an additional project. But if you have something on hand that reveals your uniqueness, by all means use it. For example, a girl interested in photography sent to Ohio Wesleyan a tasteful male pin-up calendar that she and a friend had marketed. A Tufts applicant sent copies of the school literary magazine she had edited. A young man who makes and sells intricate metal puzzles explained to the colleges why he sent one with each of his applications—"something to keep you entertained while reading essays." Two friends, both applying to Columbia, sent in a movie they had made together. One aspiring architect submitted his blueprints for a geodesic-domed city with his MIT application. The Northwestern admissions office received a poem written on a jigsaw puzzle. To read the poem, the puzzle had to be assembled. It's not clear, however, whether it was ever completed.

> Don't go too far trying to be clever. Being yourself is your best bet.

Be creative, of course. Be serious if you're serious, witty if you're witty. Just don't go too far trying to be clever. Being yourself is your best bet.

When It's Done

What a glorious feeling it will be to click the "send" button on your computer or turn your application and essay over to the U.S. Postal Service. Then sit back and rejoice. Pat yourself on the back for a job well done. It's out of your hands, so relax and wait for the momentous day when the college sends you the good news by e-mail, or the UPS or FedEx driver delivers the *fat* envelope—the one containing information about housing, courses, freshman orientation, and, of course, the letter that begins, "It gives me great pleasure to tell you that you have been accepted in the class of. . . ."

APPENDIX A.
ESSAYS IN PROGRESS

En route from first to final draft, essay writers often pause to survey the progress they've made. After writing each draft, they decide whether to continue as before, alter their course, or even start all over again. This appendix contains two sample essays somewhere on the journey to completion. Each draft is followed by notes on what the writer should do next. Notice that later drafts of each essay incorporate the suggestions for improvement. With more drafts, who knows—the writers may have produced essays to stir the blood of the most hard-hearted admissions dean.

Ellie E's First Draft

This essay responds to the "significant personal experience" question on the Common Application. Ellie wrote her first draft rather quickly—and it shows, as you will see:

> During an Outward Bound expedition in Minnesota I was put in several difficult situations. I never could have imagined them before. I was in front of a steep 80-degree incline and told to climb it to the top. My first reaction was, "There is no way I can do it." But I had no choice. I could not stay alone in the wilderness. My effort to climb the rock was the most ambitious I have ever done in my life. After two hours, I was up on the top.
>
> Even though I was there a short time, those two weeks were the most important of my life. My approach to life was different. In freshman and sophomore year I was put in many difficult academic situations. I was not making an effort. However, when I was in junior year, I made an effort. My motivation was greatly increased. Abilities I had never used before were now coming into use. My academic program was a challenge and I was meeting it gladly. With an open mind

and a willingness and a desire to try and learn, I enriched my knowledge and sharpened my skills.

I was in an honors English class with the name Modern European Literature. It was a large amount of work outside of class as well as in class discussion. The literature was difficult. I was taking the time and effort to read it until I fully understood it. In previous years, I would have dropped the class in which I was told I was going to learn about existentialism, a topic which I knew nothing about, and also write several analytical papers.

I was also challenged in math, which is one of my weaker areas. Math is not required for graduation, and I was against taking more than the least amount required to graduate. My strong dislike for the subject was keeping me from trying to learn it. But another part of me decided to meet the challenge. I didn't think it would be impossible if I made an effort. I soon found out that making the effort taught me the concepts, and logical thinking became easier for me.

Outward Bound also proved valuable in my employment. I was working as a waitress and a cashier. I had to interact with very demanding managers, co-workers, and customers. My patience was not unlimited. However, I could deal with the pressure and with others regardless of their personalities.

In the past year and a half I have shown that I can apply this new approach to my schoolwork and to everyday situations. Now I am ready to take on the responsibilities and challenges of college life and academics.

Notes to Ellie

—You have chosen a good topic, likely to impress a college, because it shows that you know what you are capable of once you put your mind to it.
—Maintain the premise of your piece, that is, how your experience in the Minnesota wilderness helped to transform you and change your attitude toward school and work. In fact, try to strengthen the cause/effect relationship.
—You attribute your sudden transformation to a single climbing experience up a steep hill. That is not plausible. To change you so dramatically, there must have been more to the Outward Bound adventure. Try to give more details. What other things occurred during those two weeks to give you a new sense of yourself?

—Your essay has good unity. You never stray from your
     topic.
—A word about your writing style. Note that most of your
     sentences use "to-be" verbs. Enliven the writing with
     more active verbs, which will also tighten the prose
     and make it more interesting to read. Also, tie ideas
     together with transitional words. Finally, combine
     sentences. Too many simple sentences tend to give
     equal weight to every idea. Try to emphasize the
     ideas that matter most.

Ellie's Second Draft

I returned from an Outward Bound expedition in
Minnesota shortly before I began my junior year. The return
was difficult as I tried to apply my new confidence to my
everyday life, including my education. In Minnesota I had
been put into several difficult situations that I never could
have imagined before. I found myself in front of a steep 80-
degree incline and told to climb it to the top. My first reaction
was, "There is no way I can do it," but I had no choice since I
could not stay alone in the wilderness. My effort to climb the
rock was the most ambitious I have ever done in my life. I
struggled for two hours, sometimes almost giving up. I felt it
might be better just to let myself roll down the hill and be
done with it. I was encouraged by others and helped by the
guide. I found the strength to go on. In the end, I stood on
the top feeling like I had truly conquered the world.

Although I had been in Minnesota only a short time, those
two weeks were the most important of my life. My motivation
to succeed had greatly increased. Abilities I had never tested
before were coming into use. My junior year in high school
was a challenge and one that I gladly met. With my mind
open, and a willingness and desire to learn, I enriched my
knowledge and sharpened my skills.

I took an honors English class entitled Modern European
Literature. It involved a large amount of work outside of class
as well as in class discussion. Although the literature was often
difficult, I took the time and effort to read it until I fully understood it. In previous years, I would have dropped any class in

which I was told I was going to read long, hard books, learn about existentialism, a topic I knew nothing about, and also write several analytical papers.

I also challenged myself in one of my weaker areas, mathematics. Because math is not required for graduation, my strong dislike for the subject tempted me to avoid it. But another part of me decided to meet the challenge. I knew it would not be impossible if I tried. I soon found out that once I made the effort to learn the concepts, logical thinking became easier for me.

The Outward Bound experience also proved valuable in my employment. Working as a waitress and a cashier, I had to interact with very demanding managers, co-workers, and customers. My patience was not unlimited. However, I managed to deal with the pressure and work, regardless of the others' personalities.

I feel that in the past year and a half I have shown that I can apply this new self-confidence and motivation to my schoolwork and to everyday situations. Now I am ready to take on the responsibilities and challenges of college life and academics.

Notes to Ellie

—This is much better than the first draft. The connection between your climb up the steep hill and your new attitude in school is much clearer now. But it could be made even stronger and more convincing if you allude to the climb in your discussion of tough courses and work experiences.

—The paragraph on your work as a waitress and cashier is still pretty vague. Either develop that paragraph further with a brief anecdote about how you coped with pressure on the job, or drop it altogether.

—Keep trying to omit needless words (notice that you reiterate the fact that the reading in your lit course was difficult).

—Keep looking for ways to combine sentences and to provide transitions between ideas, especially in the first paragraph.

Ellie's Next Draft

For two weeks during the summer between 10th and 11th grade, I participated in an Outward Bound expedition in Minnesota. Out in the wilderness with a group of teenagers like myself, I found myself face-to-face with difficult, almost unimaginable situations. I never before thought of carrying a 60-pound pack for miles on a bumpy trail or paddling a canoe 18 miles in one day. These were huge challenges for me, because I am basically an non-athlete. Until then, most of the physical challenges in my life had been optional. If I thought that I couldn't run a mile in gym class, that was the end of it; I wouldn't even try. But in Minnesota I had no choice.

One day I stood at the bottom of a very high hill with an 80-degree incline and was told to climb to the top. My first reaction cannot be printed in a college application essay, but since I could not stay alone in the wilderness, I was obligated to try. My effort to climb the rock was the most ambitious I have ever made in my life. I struggled for two hours, falling many times, getting bruised, sometimes almost giving up. At times, I stopped and felt like it might be better just to let myself roll down the hill and get it over with. But I kept on maneuvering myself upward. Others encouraged me to keep going, and the guide gave me ideas about how to proceed up huge boulders and through narrow passageways between the rocks. Somehow, I found the strength to go on. In the end, I stood on the top feeling like I had truly conquered the world. My climb had been long and exhausting, but I had done it, and maybe for the first time in my life I realized that some things that at first may seem impossible can be achieved.

Although my adventure in Minnesota lasted only a short time, those two weeks were the most important of my life. I was in a coed group of nine people, some of whom I didn't exactly like. But I learned that everyone can get along if they have to and as long as they all try. Thinking about the experience, I probably couldn't have made that climb without their help, and they couldn't have made it to the top without mine.

When I entered my junior year, I found that my motivation to succeed was changed. What I learned in Minnesota I applied to similar circumstances at work and school. The Minnesota wilderness seemed to have changed my approach to life. During my freshman and sophomore years, I often faced difficult academic situations. And like the unrun mile, I barely made an effort. I had no idea what I was missing. When the going got too rough, my motto was to give up. I had neither the tolerance nor the patience to learn or to try new things.

In 11th grade, however, I took an honors English class entitled Modern European Literature, which involved a huge amount of work. Although the literature was often difficult, I made the effort to read it until I fully understood it. In previous years, I would have dropped any class in which I was told I was going to read long, hard books and write several analytical papers. I also challenged myself in math, one of my weaker areas. Because advanced math courses are not required for graduation, my strong dislike for the subject tempted me to avoid them. But the new me decided to meet the challenge. Remembering the steep Minnesota hill, I knew it would not be impossible if I tried, and so I did and soon found out that once I made the effort to learn the concepts, logical mathematical thinking became easier for me.

The Outward Bound experience also proved valuable in my employment. Working as a waitress and a cashier, I interact with very demanding managers, unpleasant co-workers, and impolite customers. My patience was not unlimited. Again, I think of my Outward Bound group and how we all learned to get along and help each other. That's how I manage to deal with the pressure of the work. Regardless of the others' personalities, I stuck with the job and saved a few thousand dollars to help pay my college expenses.

I feel that in the past year and a half I have shown that I can apply this new self-confidence and motivation to my schoolwork and to everyday situations. Now I am ready to take on the responsibilities and challenges of college life and academics. I thank Outward Bound for that.

Notes to Ellie

—Much improved.
—You have made a strong connection between your experience in Minnesota and your recent efforts in school. The contrast between you in 10th and 11th grade and you at the present time vividly shows what Outward Bound meant to you.
—The details of the climb have added life and color to the story.

—If you can do so very, very briefly, try to relate an anecdote about a problem with a customer, a co-worker, or with your boss on the job. If you add words, though, be sure to cut words elsewhere in your essay. At the moment, the essay borders on being too long.

—Some of the essay is still a bit awkward. Read your essay aloud and listen for odd-sounding words and expressions. For example, check the verb tenses in the next to last paragraph.

In this version, Ellie seems to have overcome most of the earlier weaknesses in her essay. Of the five comments in the latest note to Ellie, only two tell her what to do next. Evidently, Ellie has taken previous suggestions to heart, and her next draft is likely to be her last.

Chuck D's Early Draft

In his essay, Chuck compares riding a bike to living in a competitive world. The idea has merit, but in this early draft Chuck may have been carried away by the uniqueness of his metaphor. Without realizing it, he has presented himself as a rather unappealing and ruthless character. He needs to view his essay with a new set of eyes before going on to write the next draft:

> The large brown garage doors of a small split-level home slowly creak open. Out emerges a ten-speed bicycle accompanied by its rider. He turns and shuts the large doors. As he mounts his bicycle, a shaft of morning sun peeks over the treetops and glistens in his face. He squints and slowly glides out of his driveway. The race has begun.
>
> He moves slowly along the street where he lives. As he approaches his first hill, he casually shifts down to first gear. Slowly but steadily he ascends the hill. As the horizon breaks, he spies a small bicycle about forty yards away. Like a cat stalking his prey, he increases his speed, legs pumping like pistons. His prey is unaware of his approach. Suddenly, his prey glances back and sees him only a few feet away, but it's too late. Our predator swiftly passes his prey.
>
> Who is this killer on a bicycle? He is me. We are one and the same. Bicycling to school is more than just a means of

transportation. It is yet another test of ability. It is a need. It is a psychological contest. Who can get there faster?

Why is this so? I feel that we in the American middle class are brought up to be competitive. When I see another cyclist who I know is going to the same place I am, I feel that I must try to beat him. While I may accomplish nothing by others' standards, in my own mind I have overcome an obstacle. In my mind, to overcome an obstacle is an achievement. I also feel if one achieves the goals which he sets for himself, he will, in his own mind be successful. While beating another bicycle to school is a small achievement, it can give you the feeling, psychologically, of a big achievement, possibly helping to pave the way to bigger and better achievements.

What are the rules which we all must follow? What might happen if we break them? The rules are: Be cool. Never let someone know that you know you are going to pass. Surprise is important. If the person doing the passing were making a lot of noise about it, one of two things could happen: He could forewarn the other person and put him on guard, making it harder for him to pass, or he would cause the person being passed to feel resentful because the person doing the passing would be too showy. Always pass someone without their knowing it. If you are passed, try to regain your ground quickly. If you can't within a reasonable period of time, don't bother. If one did not follow these rules, it would most likely have an adverse effect. If you were to let someone know you know he is passing you, then he would only get that much more joy out of seeing you helpless, or at least unable to compete with him.

As you may or may not have realized, this essay is not about riding to school. This essay is about a world filled with competition. Bicycling is just an example that illustrates just how competitive our world is, or at least how competitive my world is. In high school it has been competitive, and I'm certain it will be the same in college, if not more.

Notes to Chuck

—Good, dramatic opening. If possible, build even more tension—the kind you might feel before an important bike race.
—The race itself doesn't really begin until the rider spies his competition. Yet, you say it starts when the rider hits the street. Which is more accurate?

—Several paragraphs start with questions. The pattern gets repetitious.

—The paragraph about rules is long, confusing, and repetitive. Do you need all those rules to make your point?

—You seem driven by a personal code of ruthlessness, creating the impression that you are selfish, suspicious and sneaky. Do you want a college to think that about you? Would you want to have a friend with those qualities?

—Don't explain the point of your essay, as you do in the last paragraph. Let the essay speak for itself. Make the point forcefully enough for the reader to get it without being told.

—The basic metaphor of life as a bike race is clear, but you haven't fully explained where else in life you have experienced such intense competition.

Chuck's Next Draft

The large brown garage door slowly creaks open. Out into the morning sunshine a rider on a ten-speed emerges. He checks his helmet and the leg of his trousers. All in place. He glides silently down the drive and onto the street, pedaling slowly.

At the first hill he casually shifts down, then slowly but steadily ascends the hill. As the horizon breaks, he spies another cyclist just swinging around the corner onto the boulevard. He increases speed, legs pumping like pistons.

The race is on. He's like a cat, stalking his prey. Slowly the gap between them narrows. His prey is unaware of his approach. Suddenly, his prey glances back and sees him. But it's too late. He's by in a flash, his vanquished victim left in the dust.

Who is this speedster? Who is this cheetah of the road, outracing everyone who crosses his path? It is me. I am the unconquerable one. It's in my blood to race, to overcome, to win, even when it's just the daily ride to school.

Bicycling to school is not just a means of transportation. It is a sport, a contest to see who is fastest. It's a symptom of growing up in the great middle class of America. We have been bred on competition. From Little League to class rank, from college boards to basketball, winning always counts as the only thing that matters. Who is fastest, smartest, tallest, quickest, most popular, strongest, best looking, sexiest, most likely to succeed? Win, win, win says the wind. So, whenever I see another cyclist, I feel that I must try to beat him. It may seem like I have accomplished nothing, but to me it is another achievement, another obstacle overcome in the race of life.

I feel that if you achieve the goals you set for yourself, even the smallest ones, you will be successful in your own mind. While beating another bicyclist to school may accomplish nothing, it satisfies my longing to excel, to feel psychologically that I am better, faster and more ready to face the world.

I don't feel this competitive urge when cycling with a friend. Friends are for getting to know, not for defeating in a race. In friendship there is trust. Neither you nor your friend should feel the other's need to compete. If they feel the need, then friendship terminates, falling as a victim of mutual distrust.

So, the rules of life are like the rules of the bicycle race. Never let someone know you are coming up behind him. A warning will put him on his guard and make the passing more difficult. If you are passed, try to regain ground quickly, but if you can't within a reasonable period, don't try unless you know you can do it. It's better not to let the other person see you in distress, for he'll only get more joy out of seeing you helpless, or at least unable to compete with him. Then he may toy with you, tease you by slowing down and zooming ahead when you think you will pass him.

Long ago, Charles Darwin called it survival of the fittest. That's the way it was and always will be as long as we live in a competitive society.

Notes to Chuck

—At the start, short sentences and phrases create tension. You've hooked your reader firmly. Good!

—You've made yourself much more likeable in this version of the essay.

—You show that your competitive urges come from society, not from some dark impulse deep inside you.

—The paragraph about friendship adds another dimension to your personality.

—In this draft, you make your point clearly—and without specifically telling the reader what it is. Well done!

—This essay is almost ready to send, but not quite. Read it over carefully for unneeded words and for repetitive phrases and ideas. For instance, in the second sentence, "out" and "emerges" are redundant. Using almost identical phrases, you mention twice (sixth and seventh paragraphs) that passing the other bicyclist seems to accomplish nothing, a disclosure that you should reconsider. After all, you don't want to give readers the impression that you have uncontrollable ambition or that you are hellbent to get your way regardless of the cost. Such traits will not be received well in college admissions offices.

After some minor editing Chuck's essay will be complete, and Chuck, being a hard-core competitor, will no doubt send it off confident that it will win him a place in the college of his choice.

APPENDIX B.
COMPLETED ESSAYS

When college admissions deans curl up to read a bunch of essays, they look for answers to two key questions about each applicant:

1. What does this essay tell us about the person who wrote it?
2. What does it tell us about how well this person can write?

The second question more or less answers itself when an essay presents a clear and accurate picture of the writer. You won't find many muddled *and* well-written self-portraits. Therefore, the impression you create rests largely on how vividly you are able to project yourself onto the page.

In this appendix you'll find three college essays. Each, for better or worse, reveals the writer's personality. Before you look at the brief analysis following each essay, decide for yourself whether the essay succeeds. Put yourself in the place of a college admissions officer. What does each essay tell you about its author?

Paul G

Paul, a high school senior, put on a pair of figure skates when he was eleven and has rarely taken them off since then. He is an ice dancer. He practices hours every day, enters (and sometimes wins) competitions, and dreams of skating in the Olympics. Ice dancing consumes a major portion of his time. To convince colleges that he is more than a one-dimensional person, however, he wrote an essay titled "Achieving a Balance."

> Achieving a balance on an almost paper-thin blade of steel can be a stressful experience. The first time I fell it hurt. I think of where I was then and where I am now and see my life in between as a balancing act, much like skating is, literally. The lesson I learned from falling that first time I remember: "If you stay balanced, you won't fall."

Over the next six years I learned how to stand; strong and confident. Now, spending hours a day training, I rarely, if ever, think about falling. In the beginning it was just another new sport. Now, ice dancing is a passion. However, sometimes a passion can become a misguided devotion to only one part of life. As competition and training became more difficult, keeping life in perspective grew more challenging. Increased skating demands forced me to get better organized. My mother and I spend hours driving to rinks, so I used that time to read a lot—from Cormac McCarthy to the newest Brian Jacques (a holdover from my childhood). Through it all I remained sane by staying in conventional school (competitors typically opt for tutoring or home schooling). I made time to spend with friends, continued to play tennis and baseball (despite some skating coaches' objections to playing other sports), and I rejected the notion that skaters had to live a life secluded in a rink.

My coach and friend Mikchail Zverev taught me what ice dancing really means: to skate with a partner as one and to feel each other's every move. I learned from him how to deal with inherently subjective judging by focusing on how well I skated, and then thinking about improving my skating even more. Mikchail's life in Russia had been harsh physically and politically. Because he had experienced what it was like to lose what you love, he grasped my need for staying centered—both on ice and in life. When the training got tough, he understood and helped me get through it.

There is a fullness in life that I have enjoyed because of my skating and what it has given me. But life is not all about oneself, and last year I was given a chance to start teaching a group of underprivileged girls through a program called Figure Skating in Harlem. The cold wind off the Hudson River could not diminish my enjoyment in giving back to skating. The smiles on the girls' faces, and on mine, when they achieved something new made me relish each Saturday.

Having the talent to skate has led to tough choices, but I think that trading skating for an easier, less stressful, life would have been copping out. I chose skating but rejected the baggage that too often came with it; a narrow view of life with too little exposure to the real world. The thin steel blade that had the potential to trip up my life instead led me to balance skating with learning, with other sports, with friends and family—all of which have enriched my life.

—Paul G the person has considerable self-confidence and a sense of who he is . . . has a competitive streak in him . . . realizes the diversity that life has to offer . . . knows he has a special talent but has rejected the life of a celebrity . . . takes pride in helping others.

—Paul G the writer knows how to catch the reader with an appealing opening . . . has an original mind and the imagination of a poet . . . understands how to show his many-sided personality without writing a list . . . knows how to sustain a metaphor . . . realizes that an essay's conclusion should remind the reader of the introduction . . . shows facility in writing clear English.

Peter S

At the start of his essay, Peter addresses the admissions committee directly. Writing the essay, he feels, is like fighting a battle with an unseen enemy.

It is hard for me to believe that the crucial time has arrived when I will leave the protective world of high school and enter another world as a major contestant and participant. Applying to college is my first step as a contestant in a unique kind of battle, one that is fought without blood—only sweat and tears. You, the admissions committee, become the judges. In your heads the decisive victories are won and lost. We, the winners and losers, battle one another only in words. Our minds and souls come to you in a record of scores, letters of recommendation, and, perhaps most of all, through this essay. Here you find out about the "me" not revealed in transcripts or through others' words. Each word I write represents another piece to the puzzle of my mind. How I sympathize with you, for some of the pieces may seem confusing or not even part of the puzzle.

Initially, I tried writing an essay that explained how I have been working to improve myself as a person. I grew frustrated with the difficulty of portraying the person I would like you to know, or finding an adequate way to show you my elation over the changes and growth I have experienced, especially since last summer. Now I can picture you sitting there thinking, "Well, here is another kid trying to get into our college by telling us how he has improved as a person." To tell you the truth, that picture makes me somewhat defensive. I know what this war is about: It's essay-eat-essay.

Do you remember when you feared that each word you put down would determine your future? If I had submitted my self-improvement essay, would you have been as deeply moved as I was? Would you have dropped your jaw and danced with excitement as I did when certain events happened to me? Let me try!

I have always wanted to be a more sociable person who, on meeting new people, did not retreat into a shell. Picture me *before:* One day I was stopped at a traffic light when another car pulled alongside. Inside were three of the most gorgeous examples of "pulchritude" I have ever seen. One girl about my age turned toward me. Horror! She was looking straight at me, checking *me* out just as I had done to her! I began to get nervous. Was there egg on my face? Was it April Fools'? Then the most embarrassing thing happened. She waved at me, and what's more amazing, even had the audacity to smile. My pulse went crazy. Was this really happening to me? WOW! I sure would like to meet her. But NO! I shriveled up in my seat. The light changed, and off we went into our own worlds, never to see each other again. So why didn't I wave back? Here was the opportunity I had been waiting for, and what happened? I blew it!

This experience turned out to be a valuable lesson. I began to think, "Is this the person I want to become?"

Many months passed as I sorted out many feelings about myself. During a family vacation in the White Mountains I began to realize that I had to change things that had been part of my personality for so long. I began to experiment with a "new me" during my hikes in the mountains. Each new person I met, I greeted with a hearty "Hello" and a bubbling smile. Not even totally exhausted hikers looked unfavorably at this cheerful, outgoing lad. Then it hit me! This lad was who I really wanted to be.

The new beginning: Back at the hotel I began to worry. I did not want to lose the person whom I wanted to become. I would have to work hard to assume his identity at all times. Trying out my new personality was not always successful, and sometimes the security of my old shell seemed very inviting. But then, *Success!*

I had always wanted a job in the dining room of this hotel. On the morning of our departure, I talked with the maitre d' about the mountains, about the hotel, about the dining room, about myself. No matter. Now, I knew what I was doing. I was communicating more easily, without my previous reserve. I was enjoying myself. More importantly, I *knew* there was no egg on my face! At the end of our conversation, I asked the maitre d' if he would give me a job, and you'd never guess what he said. He said, and I quote, "I would love to have someone with your personality working in my dining room!" Well, I hit the thirty-foot ceiling!

After reading this essay, did you? Probably not, for it was difficult to convey my feelings and my thinking. But I hit it. Even if my self-improvement essay did not captivate you, I know that I have, in fact, grown.

I cannot deny the past, nor do I want to. Now I feel ready to do battle. My ammunition will come from within, and any victories, as well as any losses, will be my own. I have waged a battle with myself, and I am winning. I am liking who I am. No matter what the outcome of this contest, I will keep on growing and evolving into the person I want to be. I want to hit those thirty-foot ceilings again and again!

—*Peter S the person seems a bit unsure of himself at the start . . . grows increasingly self-confident as the essay goes on, as well as in life . . . thinks that he's misunderstood—that people don't see the sensitive, complex person residing inside him . . . has a sense of humor . . . has the capacity to change . . . has the resolve to overcome personal hang-ups . . . wants to succeed . . . is sincere . . . has the courage to reveal his anxiety . . . is blessed with charm and a gentle disposition.*

—*Peter S the writer takes risks with words and ideas . . . knows how to project his personality onto the page . . . can use an appropriate story to make a point and develop an idea . . . focuses on an important personal issue . . . demonstrates overall writing competence . . . uses sentence variety and vivid images . . . gets bogged down in wordiness occasionally . . . knows how to write a strong and memorable conclusion.*

Betsy S

Betsy portrays herself with several brief glimpses into her memory. Although the images are separated by time and space, when taken as a whole, they become a finely crafted, unified self-portrait.

Certain experiences that I've had in my life have helped to shape me, along with all my schooling and all that I've learned from other people, into the person I am today. Some of them, although they may have occurred long ago, are still so vivid to me that I feel that I could shut my eyes and be there in those places again. . . .

I grasp the lifeline with my bronzed little ten-year-old hands and stretch my toes down to touch the cold Maine water. Today is beautiful, the water is calm and glistening. The boat leaves a trail of white bubbles behind it as it glides along. We were up at sunrise, Daddy and I were. At least we were up to meet the lobster boats as they went by and we got the first pick of the morning's catch. I had taken a before-breakfast swim and now my swimsuit hangs from the boom, drying in the wind. I turn my head back, lean under the jib, and wave to my dad who sits holding the tiller with his bare foot. My mother sits near him, reading a book, my sister is sunbathing, and my little brother is playing with the hermit crabs that we've adopted as pets. My father beckons me back to the cockpit and lets me take the tiller. I stand with my bronzed, proud little ten-year-old face gazing up, over the cabin, off at the horizon . . .

The tears flow down my face, faster still as I glance at my sister and brother, their faces tearstained too. It seems so ironic to me that, at eleven years old, I am standing in the most beautiful restaurant in New York, in the most elegant dress I've ever owned, and I am experiencing the most pain I've ever felt. My father glances over his shoulder at us, even as the ceremony is taking place, and I see the pain in his eyes too. I think of my mother, alone at home, in the huge, new house that he just bought for us. What will she have done when he drops us off tonight? Last weekend she tore up their wedding picture. She's broken some dishes and called him every rotten name right in front of me. Inside I've called him them too. I'm only eleven years old and I'm so confused. I love my parents both so much and I'm not ready to have these feelings. I hardly even know this woman he's marrying . . .

I wake up, having slept for the shortest four hours of my life and I force my eyes open and I crawl to the shower as I shampoo my hair. My brain begins to function again and I think to myself, "Any sane person is going to the beach today, sleeping until noon, and wouldn't think of touching a schoolbook." After my shower, I go back to my room and Lindsey, my roommate from Toronto, and I get dressed in a hurry. Grabbing our books we run down the stairs and out the door of our dorm to walk to breakfast. On the way to the Commons, we begin to meet all our friends. It has become a daily ritual, these past weeks at Andover. First we see the kids from Stevens East and Taylor Hall hiking up the hill. Soon we see Jennifer and Dana coming across the quad from Day Hall. We walk into the Commons, grab some Cap'n Crunch and a glass of O.J. and walk over to join the others at a table. I sit back and listen to everyone. They're complaining about their homework, the lack of sleep, the food, the strict curfews, and chattering about our next trip to Boston, letters from home, the newest couple, and I smile at Lindsey and our looks say to each other, "When have we ever been this happy before?" . . .

I stand at the top and lift my face up toward the sun. I take off my sunglasses and lean forward onto my poles. I feel every muscle in my body, every muscle in my legs, my shoulders, my arms . . . A pacific, white sea lies in front of me. There's not another person around me. I'm skiing better than I ever have before. I'm concentrating on every move as if in slow motion. I feel so close to Heaven and so down to Earth. I feel a remarkable energy, maybe from the sun, maybe from the center of the Earth, flowing through me, making me glow. Everything inside me, in my head, seems to come together and I am whole. I lift my face toward the sun and I can't help but smile as I think to myself, "This is me. This is what I am."

There are so many other examples that I could choose to show who I am, many of them are not vivid images of memorable moments, but everyday parts of my life. I love to walk down the hall at school, talking and joking with almost everyone I pass, teachers and students alike. I love the feeling I get when I tutor someone and I help them to understand a concept that they couldn't quite get on their own. Most of all, I love to sit at the kitchen table and talk with my mother and her fiancé, or to go out with my close friends and laugh and hug and know that we can always lean on each other. I work hard and I play hard. I spend a great deal of time studying my books, but also a lot of time forming relationships with other people. I want all the beauty that life can give . . . all the knowledge, all the love. So I fill up my cup and I drink it in.

—*Betsy S the person loves life and appreciates its possibilities . . . feels and thinks deeply . . . searches below the surface for the essential meaning of everyday occurrences.*

—*Betsy S the writer has a rare gift for saying what she thinks and feels . . . has composed an essay that deserves to be read again and again.*

APPENDIX C.
STUDENT CONTRIBUTORS*

Elissa Greenberg Adair, Princeton

Chandra Bendix, MIT

Joel Berkowitz, University of Pennsylvania

Ian Biederman, Northwestern

Deborah Brause, Tufts

Brian Cunnie, University of Pennsylvania

Peter Davis, Johns Hopkins

Roger Denny, Columbia

Teresa DiMagno, SUNY Binghamton

Charles DiMicco, SUNY Albany

Sabrina Eaton, University of Pennsylvania

Ellie Ehrenhaft, Ithaca

Susan Epstein, Yale

Lisa Estreich, Harvard

Susan Faulkner, Brown

Ellen Gamerman, Swarthmore

Paul Goldner, Harvard

Alicia Grant, SUNY Binghamton

Maria Guarino, Fordham

Alexander Harrington, Columbia

Lawrence Harris, Franklin and Marshall

Eric Hecker, University of Pennsylvania

Elizabeth Humphrey, Fordham

Alison Lipow, University of North Carolina

Thomas Mackenzie, University of Colorado

Steven Maddox, Harvard

Jon Martin, Cornell

Sally McCauley, Smith

Pamela Meadow, University of Pennsylvania

David Miles, University of California, Berkeley

Michael Miller, New York University

Tracy Parker, Carleton

James Reilly, Duke

Annette Rogers, Boston University

Elizabeth Schmidt, University of Michigan

Peter Scotch, Connecticut College

Andrew Smith, Washington University

Gina Smith, Syracuse

Linda Wiereck, Oberlin

*Several contributors chose to withhold their names or to be listed under a pseudonym.